The Schlumpf Obsession

The Schlumpf Obsession

- inside a legendary treasure house

Denis Jenkinson & Peter Verstappen

Historical Consultant: Michael Sedgwick

Heron House Associates

Doubleday & Company Inc.

A Heron House Book
First edition in the United States of America
Published in 1978 by Doubleday & Company, Inc.,
Garden City, New York
ISBN 0 385 14409 1
Library of Congress Catalogue Number 78 50878

Filmset by
Trident Graphics Ltd,
83 Bell Street,
Reigate,
Surrey, England.

Colour reproduction by
Culver Graphics
Lane End
Bucks, England.

Printed by
Alabaster Passmore and Sons Ltd
Maidstone
Kent, England

Contributors: Denis Jenkinson and Peter Verstappen
with Michael Bowler; Drayton Bird; Tony Brignall;
Hugh Conway; Anne Delemme; Robin Dolton; John Fletcher;
Gray Joliffe;
Gerald Kemmett; Christopher Maynard

Editorial Director:
Tessa Clark

Art Director:
Tim Fitzgerald

Historical Consultant:
Michael Sedgwick

Photographers: Peter Cramer; Pascal Gerrer;
Geoffrey Goddard; Francis Hillmeyer;
Peter Lienhard; Maurice Rowe; Daniel Schmitt

CONTENTS

FOREWORD

The story of Hans and Fritz Schlumpf and the Schlumpf collection is almost unbelievable, stranger indeed than fiction. It had to be told—in the detail that it has been in this book and with its considerable accuracy and research. It is still difficult to know what conclusions to draw. The Schlumpf brothers are unusual to say the least. Their true character remains unclear.

If their story is fascinating, what of the museum at Mulhouse, and the way it has been built up?

Fritz Schlumpf was undoubtedly unwise to create his collection within the confines of his factory where it was inextricably linked with the company and its employees. No doubt anyone as autocratic as he would be insensitive to the 'unacceptable face of capitalism'. Nevertheless, the workers' reaction is understandable. Their occupation of the museum has been tolerated because at least the cars are looked after.

The most difficult assessment to make is of the museum itself: fascinating, remarkable, unique, it is, without question, well worth seeing. It is also vulgar and lacking in taste. It reminds the visitor of a *nouveau riche* extravaganza. A museum should have a message—in this case probably a message built around transport, or racing cars. It should have some sort of balance in its exhibits instead of many examples of the same model merely to show how wealthy it is. It should display its wares so that the visitor can get as much as possible out of his visit without touching the exhibits. Ropes strung feet away from the vehicles, closed doors and engine covers inhibit viewing and instruction. In some cases added bodies hide intriguing chassis details which could have been revealed.

And what a shame it was to see so many fine cars which in the hands of many collectors could still be on the road in the hands of one who would never allow them to move again.

Other museums—Harrah, Beaulieu, Le Mans—take their cars out from time to time. They even allow enthusiasts to drive them so that the public can see them being used. It is unlikely that a man like Fritz Schlumpf would ever do this. If the museum passes into other hands there may be hope.

This book is compulsive reading, whatever your view on the Schlumpf brothers. Its authors are to be congratulated on the thoroughness of its preparation.

Hugh Conway

London, June 1977

THE SCHLUMPF SAGA

In photos: signs reading "BIEN MAL ACQUIT NE PROFITE PAS", "ALPHONSE P2", "Je gagne 1830 F per mois"

The entrance to the Mulhouse museum
and two of the cars in the collection

*The textile factory at Malmerspach where
the Schlumpf collection began*

An hour before dawn on the cold, clammy morning of March 7 1977 a group of disgruntled workers trudged along the canal bank in Mulhouse, Alsace. Many were paunchy and middle-aged, an improbable group bent on an incredible raid.

Their target was one of the factories belonging to the Schlumpf brothers. A year earlier this would have been easy to spot, even in the half-light. It had always been floodlit. Now there were no lights, although it was rumoured ex-gendarmes with Alsatian dogs still patrolled the grounds.

Each man scrambled nervously over the low fence of the dark deserted villa next to the factory and into its overgrown garden. In puritanical Alsace the factory owner often lived alongside his factory—a symbol of near-feudal power over his employees.

But the Schlumpfs, Fritz and Hans, posed no immediate physical threat. This was but one of their many factories and for more than 30 years they had lived further up the valley in their personal kingdom—Malmerspach. Even there the villa had been

shuttered and locked these past ten months, bolted and inaccessible as they had bolted to their native Switzerland and were inaccessible now. The only person to contend with was a solitary guard in the sentry box.

The amateur commandos paused to muster their forces then, with an undisciplined rush across the cobbles, surrounded the guard. Their leader, Jean Kasper, a gentle, reasonable man, softly explained: "We won't hurt you, you're a worker, and the workers are taking over."

Loyalty, discipline, and fear of authority die hard in the Alsace. Fifteen men notwithstanding the guard pushed the alarm button connected to the local gendarmerie. Nothing happened. Like the rule of the Schlumpf brothers, it had broken down.

Police or no police the guard refused to give up the keys. It didn't matter. The workers scaled a ledge, found an unlocked window, and were in.

What they found was astounding, a scene viewed previously

Inside the Mulhouse museum; automotive riches as far as the eye can see

The missing element; Rembrandt Bugatti's elephant

by a mere handful of special visitors including several members of Europe's royal families: the incredible Schlumpf rare car collection.

It would take the workers some hours merely to count the cars spread over the equivalent of more than three football fields. When they finished, their tally would be 427 automobiles, virtually all in showroom condition and the majority in superb working order.

The assortment was astonishing. Cars included Hispano-Suizas, Ferraris, Mercedes-Benz, Rolls, Panhards, Renaults, Peugeots, Lancias, Isotta-Fraschinis, Alfas and Ballots in profusion, and profusion could mean lots; for example, the largest Bugatti collection in the world, 122 in total. But while the workers were looking at a completed museum, they were by no means looking at all the cars. Another 150 were stashed away in the workshops, ranging from yet more Bugattis to an exclusive 8-litre Bentley. And what the workers also could not realise was the rarity of much that they beheld.

There was a Swiss-built Dufaux eight-cylinder racing car built in 1904-1905—one of only two, its equivalent is in Lucerne's Transport Museum; and a 1912 'Alfonso' sporting Hispano-Suiza named after the King of Spain whose wife had given him an earlier model in 1909. It is as rare as it is remarkably efficient.

Bugatti's personal Type 56 electric runabout was there. He used it in the early 1930s to move about his Molsheim factory. So was an exceptional Gordini sports-racer, one of the earliest of Gordini's cars, built from Simca-Fiat components. Gordini sold it in 1938 to a fellow Italian named Molinari who preserved it faithfully until after the war. After his death his will revealed that, in a remarkable gesture of appreciation, Molinari had left the car to Gordini so it returned to the Paris factory.

There was a 1937 Mercedes-Benz W 125 Grand Prix car converted for mountain hill climbs after the 1937 Grand Prix season; only two such models are known in the world. Like its sister car, in the 1950s it was smuggled out of Eastern Europe.

In the centre of the collection stood the crown gems: two of the world's six Bugatti Royales, the Coupé Napoleon and the Park Ward, each in perfect working order yet missing one tiny element—the radiator caps including the Park Ward's graceful silver elephant sculptured by Rembrandt Bugatti at his brother Ettore's request. Fritz Schlumpf couldn't remove the cars but he could take their ornaments.

The hall, once a textile factory, had a saw-toothed roof which provided natural light. The roof was supported by 800 iron pillars each of which held reproduction candelabra modelled after those found on Venice's Grand Canal. Broad aisles, named after members of the Schlumpf family, stretched across the hall.

Alongside the museum lay three incredible restaurants, one Italian, one Parisian, and one Swiss. Together they seated 1200. They had Louis XV chairs and gilt chandeliers, even the toilets had gilt mirrors. The restaurants were decorated with early carts and, inset in the wall, were brass portholes which displayed the Schlumpfs' own private champagne.

Within an hour the take-over was complete. By 9 o'clock

Left: *Bugatti Type 49; an elegant
3.3-litre eight-cylinder coupé*

Below: *Mercedes 28/95 tourer*

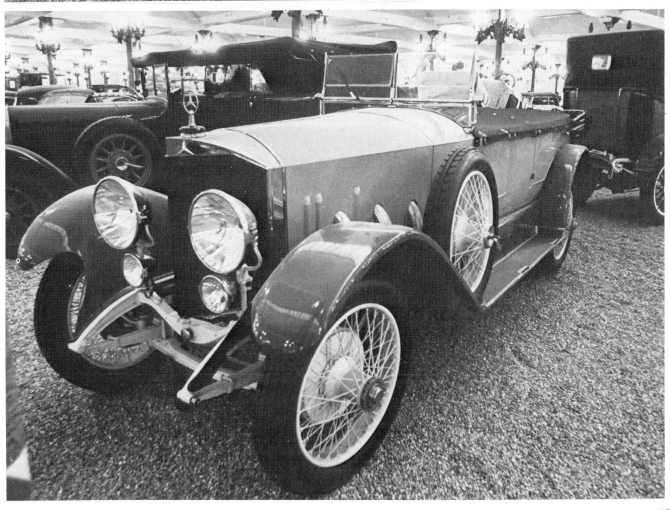

Above: *One of the collection's priceless Bugatti Royales carrying a written protest from a Malmerspach worker. Veteran cars form a backcloth*

Far right: *Supporting lamp posts are of incredible opulence*

Right: *'Champers' chez Schlumpf*

workers were manning the switchboard and the gate. As the day progressed cars and buses brought workers from the other Schlumpf factories at Erstein, Malmerspach and Roubaix to see the newly proclaimed *Workers' Museum*, "the fruit from the sweat of our brows".

Commanding the whole scene at the entrance way is a tableau entitled, *"A notre chère maman"*. It commemorates Jeanne Schlumpf (1878-1957) to whom the entire collection is dedicated. The tableau is possibly a clue to the Schlumpf obsession. This powerful woman exerted an extraordinary influence on her unconventional sons.

The Early Days

Hans Schlumpf was born on February 21 1904 (when Bugatti was 25). Fritz arrived almost exactly two years later on February 27 1906. Both were born in Omegna, a small town near Milan. Their father, Carl, was Swiss and worked for a textile firm. Their mother, Jeanne, had been born in Mulhouse on June 25 1878. Because Alsace was then German the boys could claim dual Swiss-German nationality later on. This was to prove useful.

19

Top: *Even the mirrors in the toilets are gilt-edged*

Above: *"The collection will be in memory of my mother. It's unique."*

Right above: *Fritz in the driver's seat*

Right: *Part of the interior of one of the museum's three restaurants*

In 1908 the family moved to Mulhouse, where Carl again worked in textiles while sending both boys to school. While Alsace is predominantly Lutheran, the family was devoutly Catholic and Hans was educated by the Christian Brothers in Switzerland. On his return he went to the Mulhouse Lycée and completed his studies at the city's Ecole de Commerce, where he received a Diploma in Commercial Science.

Fritz attended the same *lycée* but ended his studies after matriculation. The death of their father in August 1918 possibly explains this, as the family may have fallen on hard times.

In the early 1920s Hans apprenticed as a banker while Fritz began trading in coal before going into textiles as a broker.

Apparently Fritz was good at it. By 1928, at the age of 22, he already owned his own Bugatti which he raced in the Ballon d'Alsace hill climb of that year.

By the late 1920s the brothers were working together on woollen deals, but their lives did have more racy aspects. Fritz was travelling, and on a trip to Berlin in 1933 he met Paule Erny, a minor figure in Berlin's *demi-monde*. She quickly became a major figure in his life; Paule figured in the lives of many men.

By 1936 she was back in Paris. It was there that she was spotted at a dance hall by Raoul Simha, a Greek-Jewish textile dealer, who bet a friend that he could get her to bed that night. He won, and that brief encounter was to have long-range consequences in the lives of the Schlumpf brothers.

In October 1935 the brothers, by now living with their mother on the Rue de la Sinne in Mulhouse, started their first formal business venture together. It was a brokerage company, the Société Anonyme pour l'Industrie Lainère and dealt in raw wool.

From the outset Hans was the inside man, handling finance and details, while the ebullient Fritz was the company's public face—a salesman of formidable persuasion with an exceptionally dominating personality.

The brokerage brought Fritz into contact with the wool mill at Malmerspach, La Filature de Laine Peignée de Malmerspach S.A., which processed their wool for export. In 1936 the brothers began to acquire stock in the mill and by October 1938, Fritz was on the board.

1938 was a banner year for Fritz. On December 17 he married Paule Erny and promptly installed her in the house on the Rue de la Sinne with Maman. Predictably, mother and daughter-in-law loathed one another from the outset. So, in an unusual arrangement, Fritz moved his bride to Paris visiting her at weekends after working during the week in Mulhouse.

By late 1939 Fritz had both a triumph and a tragedy on his hands. He was appointed managing director at Malmerspach but he also became the father of a retarded child. In February the following year the Malmerspach board of directors voted to increase the mill's share capital from ten to fifteen million francs. A new stock issue of 2000 shares was to be offered on the Bourse at Nancy to existing shareholders. The option period extended from April 10 to May 10. Hans and Fritz took 1900 of the 2000 shares and in doing so acquired effective control of the mill. Hans joined the board.

Bugattis featured in the museum and in the brothers' living room

Inset: *Maman; her influence was formidable, so was she*

22

Hans (left) *and Fritz* (right) *under attack*

The war had had little visible effect on the brothers, but on the day the share option period closed France was invaded.

Earlier in May, M. Matter, the local sub-prefect, had sent a top-secret memorandum to the prefect of the area. It recommended that Fritz be deported back to Switzerland (the brothers' native country by dint of their father's nationality). The grounds were extreme Nazi sympathies. However, the Swiss Consul in Mulhouse, Walter Kunz, objected and the move was foiled.

By June, France had fallen and Alsace was annexed to Germany. With the occupation in Paris Fritz sent his wife and child to Pyla-sur-Mer, a beach resort in the Vichy free zone.

Under German rule the brothers role was controversial but on balance highly favourable. Their factories flew both the Nazi and Swiss flags and the brothers organised the first Nazi ideological meetings in the district in their company. And when the bomb attempt was made on Hitler's life, the following telegram was despatched from Malmerspach on July 27 1944:

ADDRESS OF LOYALTY TO THE FUHRER OF GREATER GERMANY. AT A SPECIAL MEETING CONVENED AT MALMERSPACH JULY 27 1944 BY THE MANAGING DIRECTOR AND WORKERS' REPRESENTATIVE OF THE FILATURE DE LAINE PEIGNEE DE MALMERSPACH, THE WORKERS OF THE LABOUR FRONT AND THE POLITICAL LEADERS DEPLORE THE COWARDLY ATTEMPT ON THE LIFE OF THE FUHRER ADOLF HITLER, A CRIME AGAINST THE GERMAN PEOPLE IN ITS GRIM STRUGGLE FOR SURVIVAL. IN THE NAME OF ALL THE WORKERS THEY CONGRATULATE THE FUHRER ON HIS MIRACULOUS ESCAPE AND PLEDGE THEIR WHOLEHEARTED CONTRIBUTION AND EXEMPLARY ATTITUDE UNTIL FINAL VICTORY.
SIGNED
THE MANAGING DIRECTOR: SCHLUMPF
THE WORKERS' REPRESENTATIVE: GROB

But these were matters of convenience not of conviction. The Schlumpfs' real feelings are more accurately revealed by their 1942 company report. It refers to three pre-war workers who died fighting the Nazi invasion as "fallen on the field of honour" while saying merely that five employees who voluntarily joined the Waffen S.S. had been "killed in the East".

All managing directors were required to close their letters to their Nazi superiors "Heil Hitler". Fritz refused. When his superior put pressure on· him to do so Fritz simply stopped corresponding with him for the balance of the war. Fritz's·

admirers, and there are many, cite this as a strong point in his favour. His detractors, and there are more, say that he simply refused to acknowledge that any person could be superior to him, even Hitler.

Even in these troubled times the brothers derived great enjoyment from overdoing things. For example, the room in which the Nazi meetings were held was filled with enormous banners to the point of caricature, while there was only a minute statuette of Hitler at one end. Fritz and Hans quietly warned all their workers to be careful whenever Nazi officials or known sympathisers were about. As Fritz put it: "If the boss is willing to act like a clown the least I can expect from the workers is that they'll toe the line."

Loyalties apart, Fritz liked his creature comforts. When he went to Paris he stayed at the Grand Hotel, normally reserved for Nazi dignitaries. He had good occasion to go. His wife Paule had returned from Pyla-sur-Mer and was living in a flatlet at 72 Boulevard de Courcelles, quite near the Arc de Triomphe. She had many lovers including a young German officer known only as Klaus and her old flame, Raoul Simha, who by now was trading with Fritz. Fritz's child had not accompanied her. Marielle had been placed in a Swiss home for the mentally retarded where she received excellent care.

Simha had fallen hopelessly in love with Paule and was a jealous man. He and Paule quarrelled bitterly, often in public. A major point of contention was Paule's continued willingness to sleep with Fritz on weekends. She was generous by nature and refused to cede the point.

Fritz was aware of this situation yet tolerated it. As he stated in the trial that was to come years later: "I was ready to put up with anything in order not to lose the mother of my child."

Fritz, Simha and Paule went out together frequently, yet for both men it appears to have been an unsatisfactory *ménage à trois*. Simha felt he could take it no longer and begged Paule to leave Fritz. She refused and he, in spite of the danger of being Jewish in wartime Paris, stormed into the Nazi-infested Grand Hotel and confronted Fritz. Simha demanded that if Fritz would not give her up at least he should "look after her and stop her promiscuous ways." It did not work, as Fritz was touchingly to testify later: "I always believed that loving a woman was not just keeping her to yourself but also meant giving her the happiness she expects."

In 1942, Simha was picked up by the Gestapo. He was transported to LeDrancy, north of Paris, a holding pen for those awaiting deportation to labour camps or the final solution.

Incredibly, at Paule's request Fritz interceded. He dealt with both the Gestapo and the French Ministry of the Interior, and was successful. Simha was mysteriously released.

At the close of the war the brothers were detained several times on suspicion of collaboration. Ultimately, with much favourable evidence from their employees, they were cleared. Thereafter they could concentrate on the business and their new-found hobby—dabbling in old cars.

Their first known post-war acquisition had all the audacity and

Bugatti Type 101, with bulbous drophead coupé body

farsightedness of the boom collecting years (1957-1973). They bought a French Talbot from General de Lattre de Tassigny, the very man who had been the overall regional commander when they had been detained. The car was bought in classic Schlumpf style using a Swiss journalist as a 'blind' intermediary and, typically, they had had their eye on it for sometime. It had been a Nazi staff car in Mulhouse.

Murder Will Out

"My honeybun told me 'I've killed my lover'. I said, 'Quel malheur' ". Statement by Fritz Schlumpf in the trial of Paule Schlumpf for first degree murder, November, 1948.

While the war was over one thing hadn't changed. Paule Erny still had what the prosecution at the trial were to call "La cuisse légère"—'easy thighs', and she still had Raoul Simha as one of her lovers although the affair was coming to an end.

Just who was going to end it is a matter of dispute. At the

subsequent trial the defence claimed Paule wanted out at any cost while the prosecution said it was Simha, but first there was the matter of a substantial sum of money and a diamond that Madame Schlumpf wanted rather badly. Only one thing is totally clear—matters resolved themselves with a bang.

On August 4 1946 Paule arranged to swap apartments with an old friend, Madame Bricout. Thus early morning on August 5 found Paule and Raoul Simha in residence at 8 Rue du Saigon.

Simha was naked and quite suddenly, Simha was dead. Paule claimed that they had quarrelled violently and she had then mistaken his reaching for a cigarette as reaching for a gun. As a result, she said, she'd shot him in self-defence.

The story had a certain implausibility. There was the matter of where the bullet had entered the body—at the base of the back of the skull.

Paule wasted no time in attempting to cover her movements. She first called Madame Bricout to urge her to come over since "there'd been trouble." Together they attempted, and failed, to dress the corpse (Simha was a heavy man). Next she went to the Bois de Boulogne and disposed of the weapon. Finally she called her weekend husband, Fritz Schlumpf.

He arrived at ten that evening. Together they dressed the corpse, then he took her straight to France's most renowned criminal lawyer, Maitre René Floriot. Floriot advised that she give herself up at once and plead self-defence.

The Paris police didn't accept the plea. She was gaoled in the Petite Roquette prison and, French justice grinding exceedingly slow, her trial opened on November 27 1949, over 27 months after the event.

The Parisian popular press had a field day and Paule was nothing if not obliging. She dressed in a dark suit which featured a plunging neckline, topped this with a mink, and cropped her hair short like Greta Garbo's, with whom she was constantly compared.

She was pronounced guilty and sentenced to eight years. Fritz had stood by her throughout the long ordeal. Now he felt free to divorce her and promptly did.

Mother and Malmerspach

There was still very much a Madame Schlumpf in the lives of Fritz and Hans.

Maman was a tyrant, but the boys adored her. An enthusiasm not shared by domestic staff in the villa. The turnover was astonishing. Maids and cleaning women lasted an average of two weeks; when one stuck it out for years, the locals regarded it as miraculous. The same situation prevailed in the kitchen. The Schlumpfs liked simple fare—plain ham and tomatoes was a staple ingredient of their diet. But they also knew exactly how they liked their food, which was not, apparently, how most chefs prepared it.

Ultimately the family decided that they were never going to find a cook of whom they could approve and the canteen cook, M. Untereiner handled their food.

The brothers' home life was noteworthy in other ways. Fritz had had an enormous panorama of Malmerspach painted. All those properties owned by the Schlumpfs, over 60 percent of the town, were accurately depicted including their windows. Those properties not owned by the Schlumpfs were painted without windows. As the brothers constantly acquired property the painter was frequently summoned to add new windows.

The house's furnishings were unusual in other respects. Where one would expect to find a couch there was instead a baby Bugatti. For, while Fritz had not yet entered on a collecting binge, he was already inordinately fond of cars. One of the sheds at Malmerspach housed virtually all the cars he had owned as well as several antique fire engines. A collection which, while relatively small, represented a feat in itself, since during the closing days of the war, the Germans had requisitioned everything that had wheels.

Maman was reclusive by nature. The chauffeur was sent for every purchase, but even so she was well known for her miserly ways. Once when she dispatched the chauffeur to get three pins

and he returned with a pack of ten, she sent him back to get a refund on the unnecessary seven.

The brothers' villa, partly obscured by trees

Being entertained *chez* Schlumpf had its unusual aspects. There was of course Schlumpf champagne; a little pretentious since the brothers did not own a vineyard. They simply bought enough to allow the dealer to glue on their own label.

Then there were the deer which the brothers bought to surround the villa. At first they were all the same breed, Sikas, then the brothers came across other specimens of different breeds which could be had at bargain prices.

Finding bargains hard to resist they snapped these up. The inevitable result was interbreeding which produced, as one local put it, "the mangiest deers in Christendom."

Oblivious to this the brothers would hide workers in the bushes when entertaining company. Their job was to shoo the deer into view when the guests came on to the terrace after dinner. Deer on demand, as it were.

The brothers had other animals. At one time the mill was infested with rats. They solved this by bringing in 150 cats. This led to the acquisition of a flock of goats. Their milk was given to the cats and their grazing on the company lawns eliminated the need to mow; a perfect ecological arrangement.

Maman became even more reclusive after she broke her thigh in her later years. Thereafter, much of her time was spent in her bedroom spying with binoculars on all who came into sight.

Alphonse Kublar remembers one such occasion. While working on the villa's roof he took a bucketful of rubble through the adjoining garden. On the way back he picked and ate a radish. Maman promptly reported this to head office and Hans cycled over to threaten Kublar with dismissal.

The Wool Family

It would be hard to imagine more paternalistic employers than Hans and Fritz. They ran the mill much as it must have been run by its founder, Jacques Hartmann, in the 1880s. In fact Hartmann looked somewhat like Fritz, and Fritz kept his portrait behind his desk. Visitors were not discouraged from believing it was the portrait of an ancestor. The atmosphere at the factory was feudal. Workers were forbidden to talk unless about work, the slightest sign of idling could lead to dismissal, smoking was strictly forbidden, and all workers were on a piecework basis, paid only for what they produced.

Hans was totally in charge of the daily running of the works. (Fritz almost never appeared on the shop floor) and all decisions had to be referred to Hans as he bicycled from one building to another.

He was suspicious by nature and had several favourite tricks. One was to announce that he was going elsewhere, pedal slowly out the door, then do a quick U-turn the moment he was out of sight, shift into high gear and pedal furiously back into the building in the hope that he'd catch someone in a forbidden act.

By law, the workers were allowed a 20-minute lunch break. The Schlumpfs resisted this for some time. Finally, they gave in and announced magnanimously that there would be a 30-minute break. Unfortunately, there was a catch. At the end of the day the workers had to make up the 30 minutes.

Jobs were rigorously compartmentalised so one worker might never know what the next man did. There were holes cut in the roof so workers could be spied on and, as a matter of policy, ex-gendarmes were employed since they proved to be disciplined workers and excellent informers.

Incredibly for an enterprise of its size, neither brother had a secretary. They simply didn't want anyone to know too much. Instead they employed a typing pool next to their offices. As one woman remembered: "It was like a slave ship there, constant tension, constant work, and terrible temper tantrums if we rested for just one moment."

If workers were subservient and stayed out of the union they could expect all kinds of benefits including interest-free loans and cheap housing (cheap both in terms of quality and rent).

The houses directly adjoined the works and left much to be desired. They were painted, as the workers put it, the colour of caca d'oie (goose manure), and had outdoor toilets, concrete in the case of those which faced the highway and could be seen; shanty-town wood in the case of those which faced inwards.

Workers viewed these perks with a certain jaundice. The local

Above right: *The Mulhouse workshops; colourful goings-on in drab surroundings*

Right: *Coming into Malmerspach; feudal ways on the N66*

Far right: *The Malmerspach mountain goats: "waste not, want not"*

saying was: "If you are obedient the Schlumpfs will give you anything . . . anything but a raise."

The one unpardonable sin was to leave. Fritz and Hans simply found this intolerable. For example, the two brothers ran an extensive private bus service throughout the surrounding regions. This carried workers to and from work. As a gesture of local goodwill drivers were allowed to pick up anyone going the same way—unless they happened to be an ex-Schlumpf worker. Picking up one of these meant instant dismissal. The brothers' attitude was simple—if you leave us, you can walk.

However the brothers sometimes acted as model citizens and patrons. Scarce hospital equipment and medicines obtained during the war were used when they funded two hospitals at significant expense at the end of the war. But even here the brothers could show their mean side. When a worker was about to give birth—the majority of the labour force was female—one of the brothers would act as a personal ambulance service. But he would promptly bill the government health service.

Immediately after the war the Communist trade union, the CGT, began to organise some of the workers. Surprisingly this did not trouble the brothers too much. They simply bought off the shop stewards with cushy jobs and extra pay. For a long time the Schlumpfs paid wages that were comparatively generous, though over the years this situation changed dramatically.

Above left: *Workers' houses; the plumbing changed depending on the public's view*

Left: *The new union couldn't be bought*

Above: *The brothers inspired fiery emotions; their effigies were put to the torch in 1971*

After the uprising of 1968 the Socialist union, the CFDT, increasingly took over from the Communists. Hans and Fritz found the new shop stewards could not be bought.

Neither brother had bothered to attend and chair the management-worker committees that were required by law. The result was that there was simply no consultation between management and employees. By 1971 matters had reached an impasse and the workers struck for better pay and conditions. When the brothers failed to back down there were ugly confrontations. Both factory and villa were picketed and the Schlumpfs fled to Switzerland.

The standstill had a serious effect on the Alsatian economy. Because more than 2000 jobs were at stake the region's prefect became involved. He requested a meeting, but the Schlumpfs imperiously insisted that the only place they would deign to see him was the no-man's-land of Basle Airport, strategically located in neutral territory between the two countries. Such was their power that the prefect agreed.

Ultimately the strike was settled but things were never the same. Neither of the brothers visited the factory floor again. All communications with the workers were conducted through minions or by phone.

A close feudal relationship with the workers, disaffection by them as the state supplanted the proprietor in providing social services, a bitter strike followed by the owner refusing to deal directly with the workers—it all formed a classic pattern for this part of the world. One precedent is worth keeping in mind. Ettore Bugatti had acted similarly in 1936.

Elegant Bugatti Type 57 coupé with unusual pillarless windscreen

The Collecting Years

"I've always loved cars, I've a soft spot for them. I adore beautiful machinery. It's a real passion with me and I can't explain it." Fritz Schlumpf to a friend.

The brothers had always been interested in collecting and as the 1940s ended, they had begun to assemble a wide variety of objects. Cars were one subject but by no means the only one. They collected statuary, mantlepieces, kayaks and, curiously, mounted antlers.

Fritz had acquired a Type 57 Bugatti shortly after the war, and drove it occasionally. But Bugattis were of no special interest at this time and he subsequently sold the car, much to his regret in later years.

The Schlumpfs did have other cars but most appear to have

Above: *Fritz racing round the bend*

Above right: *Deer in the grounds of the Schlumpf villa*

Right: *The brothers were fanatical collectors*

been for personal use. Such was the case in the early 1950s when Fritz imported a Buick 8. He was so excited about its arrival that he personally went down to collect it. It was to be his pride and joy for the next four years. Once he caught one of his workers peeking into the garage at it and fined him on the spot, not for being nosey, but for wasting time.

Fritz's admiration for that car is puzzling when one examines the collection in the museum today. There is not one single North American car—not a Duesenberg, a Pierce-Arrow or a Packard. Clearly geography has played an important part in their automotive interest.

1957 was a landmark year. During the summer Fritz's sporadic racing career came to an end when a workers' delegation asked Maman to see that he retired from racing on the reasonable grounds that if he went up in flames so would their jobs. Then on March 21 Maman Schlumpf died aged 78.

The funeral was grandiose, with virtually the entire staff turning out and journeying to Mulhouse where Maman was

buried in the family plot. Interestingly, the funeral procession is one of the only two known times when Fritz and Hans drove together. They usually avoided this for fear of an accident.

There were other interests also which kept them apart. Hans had a hankering for the girls in the factory. Girls who were obliging could do rather well. One was set up with a local fruit and vegetable shop and subsequently staked to a small shop in Basle. However, his philanderings could have unpleasant consequences. On one occasion he was confronted in the office by a girl brandishing a pistol.

Perhaps with this in mind Fritz sought his amusements elsewhere. A favourite spectator sport was all-in-wrestling.

Fritz had also begun to collect cars. It is impossible to know how large the collection was at this point, but it was beginning to overflow the available space at Malmerspach. The problem was solved in July 1957 when the brothers bought the spacious abandoned factory buildings of Heilman-Koechlin-Desaulles in the Avenue de Colmar at Mulhouse.

Top: *1902 Serpollet steam-powered racing car*

Right: *The Schlumpf collection's 1903 Serpollet*

Fritz was then 51 and was looking for new worlds to conquer. A magnificent collection of antique automobiles was alluring for a variety of reasons. By concentrating on Bugatti it would honour his native Alsace, where Bugatti built his cars; creating the collection would put him in touch with the rich and famous; and the collection itself would be a tangible expression of the success he and his brother had enjoyed and, importantly, a fitting tribute to their much-missed mother.

By 1958 the Schlumpfs had converted a building adjacent to the Avenue de Colmar factory into an additional workshop for restoring the cars and had installed a staff of ten. To a certain extent the workforce itself dictated that the brothers would continue to collect.

The earliest automobiles were largely made of wood; thus expert carpenters and joiners had to be employed. Many of the cars had missing or seriously defective upholstery; this required expert saddlers. Master mechanics were hard to come by; when they found one (often upon his retirement from one of the great builders) the Schlumpfs cherished him. These men required apprentices, and once they had been trained at the Schlumpfs' expense, the brothers were loath to lose them.

One of Fritz's earliest acquisitions was a Serpollet steam automobile. He had his works supervisor, Jean Joulou, devote an inordinate amount of time towards its restoration. It was secretly shipped from Malmerspach to Mulhouse for months of work on

the chassis. Then the entire machine was shipped back. Two *Bugattis in profusion*
mechanics, André Eglinger and Antoine Gieder, spent a year on
the boilers repairing the intricate brass and copper tubing.

The launching ceremony for the restorations was unvarying.
The cars had to go a minimum of 100 metres in first gear.
Unfortunately the fuel they used in the Serpollet was normally
kept for lamps and the black smoke could be seen for miles. Fritz
could not bear to watch, fearing the machine was about to
destroy itself. When the smoke died down, the chauffeur, Robert
Claden, climbed behind the wheel and made a circuit of the
yard. Only then did Fritz appear to say: "Okay, now take it to
bits again, clean it, and put it together again." The assembled
mechanics who had already spent nearly two years on the car
were left with another two months' work.

From the outset the brothers were extraordinarily secretive
about what was in the collection. However, the fact that there
was a collection was well known in the region and of itself
generated offers of additional cars.

In this way the brothers built up an extensive network of
dealers. The Schlumpfs had an edge on other collectors for three
important reasons. They were indiscriminate in what they
acquired; the market was depressed; and they were willing to
pay well over the odds. In the late 1950s a Type 35B Bugatti in
excellent condition could be had for well under £1000; ten
years later its price had quadrupled.

The Schlumpfs also outraged other collectors because the cars were being removed from public view and "they didn't seem serious." They neither worked on the cars themselves, nor did they drive them.

Feeling against the brothers was epitomized at a meeting of the British Bugatti Owners' Club at Prescott hill climb, near Cheltenham. Hugh Conway, a Bugatti expert, recalls that a tent boldly labelled 'The Anti-Schlumpf Club' was erected. Someone took a photograph of the tent and mailed it to Fritz, and Conway was *persona non grata* for some time.

Conway, a courtly and imposing Canadian, is in many ways a central figure in the Schlumpf story. He trained as an engineer then went on to have a highly successful business career with Rolls-Royce. Bugattis have been a labour of love for many years.

In late 1962, as a result of his researches he published, for his club, a register of Bugatti owners. The register electrified Fritz. In due course letters in broken English were dispatched to everyone asking if their cars were for sale. This was often done on a one-entry one-letter, two-entry two-letter, basis (perhaps because of the infamous typing pool system), almost as if the cars themselves were the recipients. Thus many owners received several letters.

As Conway puts it: "Much correspondence began to buzz mainly from the USA asking 'who is this guy' (Schlumpf) and the arguments started. Those who replied asking what they thought a silly price, only to find that they were offered about 90 per cent of it, usually fell and have been apologizing . . . ever since."

Nearly 200 unrestored cars are still hidden away

In fact the very secretiveness of the Schlumpfs worked to their advantage. When an antique car collector found himself in an embarrassing financial position he knew where to turn, and that his sale need never become public knowledge.

While many Bugatti devotees reviled the name Schlumpf, this dislike was by no means universal. Fritz had his fast firm friends and admirers in the world of motor racing. One longstanding friend was, and is, Amédée Gordini. This friendship was to benefit the museum significantly.

When Gordini gave up racing in the late 1950s and went to work for Renault, his Paris factory had all his old and current racing cars. These he generously dispersed to museums throughout France including Rochetaillée-sur-Soane, Le Mans and Chateauroux. The bulk of the collection, including such gems as the last two cars he built, the eight-cylinder Grand Prix cars of 1955 and 1957, went to Fritz. As part of the deal the cars were put in perfect working order at the Gordini factory, thus giving the workers extra time before they had to leave or move to Renault with Gordini.

While the *cognoscenti* generally regarded Fritz as simply a collector on a massive scale, he was not above doing some shrewd trading. Thus in 1962 he wrote to Conway: "During last year 15 Bugattis have left my collection." When Daimler-Benz wanted some veteran cars for their Stuttgart museum, the Schlumpfs supplied them in exchange for one of the spectacular 300 SLR sports-racers from 1955 which is still in the collection.

By the early 1960s the hunt for cars for the museum was on

1957 2½-litre eight-cylinder Gordini Grand Prix racing car

Above: *Hans and Arlette in front of Fritz; one occasion when women didn't follow behind*

Below: *John W. Shakespeare (far right) arranging to ship his collection with Southern Railway officials*

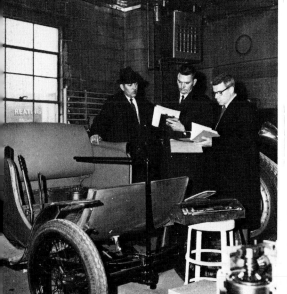

with a vengeance. Hugh Conway cared deeply about automobiles and at no profit to himself he would go to great lengths to find a car a good home. The Schlumpfs had decided to house an unparalleled automobile collection. The correspondence between them was voluminous and reflects Fritz's acquisitive ways.

Thus, Fritz to Conway in November 1962:

"I confirm that I am always a buyer of Bugatti and beg you to put me in touch with anyone in your acquaintance who is likely to sell. Can you also tell me if the 3.3 litres which was shown at the Dorchester Hotel in London and which is shown on page 274 of your latest Bugatti book is for sale.

Also, I would like to buy a series of antique and vintage cars which are the most representative of English cars, like the ones to be found in the little book which you were kind enough to send me, 'Vintage Motor Car' pocket-book—and I would be most obliged to you if you could procure and then send me photographs, technical descriptions and prices."

Not only was Fritz's appetite for cars large, it was also ambitious. From the same letter:

"What happens to the Rolls belonging to the Royal Family of England? I suppose they have to be sold from time to time. Do you have any contacts for these?"

Conway and his wife visited the museum in late 1962. Fritz initially refused to let Eva Conway in but when Conway stood firm Schlumpf relented grudgingly: *"Mrs Conway can follow on behind us."*

42

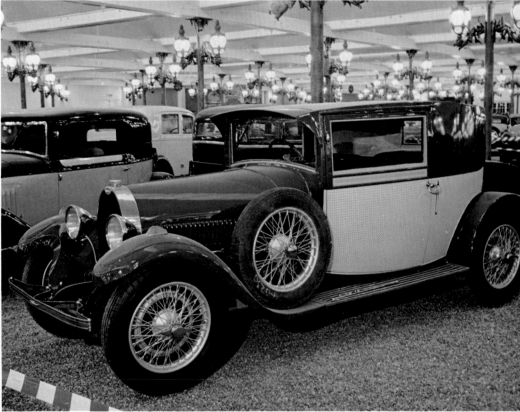

Conway has other tales from his trip. When he and his wife visited Fritz and his girlfriend, Arlette Naas, at their lakeside summer home he walked into the ground floor to find that perfectly ordinary furnishings were interspersed with racing cars. On the second floor he found a Ferrari instead of furniture sitting in the corner. Conway didn't remark on this. Neither did Fritz.

Cars from the Shakespeare collection:

Above left: Bugatti Type 55

Above: Bugatti Type 44

The Shakespeare Collection

Late in 1962 the Schlumpfs hit the jackpot. John Shakespeare, a wealthy American dealer in imported cars, had assembled an incredible collection. As Hugh Conway puts it: "I heard that Shakespeare wanted to sell the collection of 30-odd Bugattis given in the register (including the Park Ward Royale) as one lot, for the $105,000 he had paid for them." Conway wrote to Fritz on December 10. The reply was immediate:

Below: Shakespeare behind the wheel of his eight-valve 1913 Bugatti

"Dear Sir, On my return last night at 10 o'clock, I found your letter of 10th inst, which surprised me as much as it gave me pleasure.
I immediately telegrammed you this morning at 8 o'clock the following text to tell you that Mr. Shakespeare's collection interests me and that we are going to try to make this deal:

COLLECTION OF SHAKESPEARES INTERESTS ME. WILL YOU TELEGRAPH HIM TO RESERVE IT. LETTER FOLLOWING.

In any case, I want to have immediately:
A detailed list of all the cars
A description of the state of each car, from the point of view of mechanical condition and bodywork.
List of spare parts.
Numbers of motors and of chassis.

One or more photographs of each car.
The cars must be in perfect working order from mechanical and bodywork point of view.
The price of $105,000 is too much. I think I would settle on $70,000 on condition that the cars were, as I already told you, in perfect condition and that the sale be effected CIF Le Havre. The opening of credit could be done in New York, and payable against delivery of travel documents, usable one or more times.
I would like to go and see this collection myself but I do not have the time.
I suppose that you know Mr. Shakespeare and that he is a man of honour. If this is not the case, we will have to send someone. Who?
Do you have the time to go in my stead?
It is obviously necessary that the person who goes is a person in whom one can have complete confidence, because, as you wrote to me recently, there are a lot of bandits in this field of car salesmen.
I insist that these cars must be in perfect condition.
I would particularly like a lot of details on the Royale, and to have absolute confirmation that this car is in perfect working order, and that it is impeccable from a mechanical point of view as well as its bodywork. I thank you for your good news and beg you to believe dear sir, in the renewal of my best wishes.''

The cars between St Louis and the port of New Orleans; a rolling history of Bugatti which attracted spectators all along the route

Once the negotiations were joined, there was, as Conway puts it, "horse trading, angry words, changes of mind by Mr Shakespeare, threats and a bit of lubrication from me."

In looking back on the deal Conway was to reflect: "I hope that neither of the Mr Ss think I made anything out of this business—it seemed to me the friendly thing to put a buyer and a seller in touch. At one point I wished I hadn't and started thinking of seeking legal advice myself."

In due course the cars were dispatched via special train from Illinois to New Orleans and put on board a Dutch freighter bound for Le Havre. The sale attracted world-wide attention. Fritz waited impatiently and when the cars arrived in Mulhouse under heavy wraps, he had a whip to keep away the curious.

More good luck was to follow. The Bugatti factory was sold to Hispano-Suiza in mid-1963; the firm was under-financed and desperately needed money. Fritz suggested that rather than extend their overdraft he would buy the entire historic collection of 14 cars for £50,000.

As Conway relates: "Neither the boss at Molsheim, Demade, nor Roland Bugatti wanted this to happen and suggested to me that we would find someone in Britain to match Schlumpf's offers. Although we tried hard and did in fact get preliminary offers which totalled about £25,000, this was not enough and Schlumpf eventually got the lot."

Fritz and friend. This Bugatti Type 46S was bought virtually new in 1960

Above: *Bugatti Type 51 twin-cam Grand Prix car*

Right: *A magnificent period Marchal headlamp*

In little more than a year, the brothers had acquired two Royales and 42 additional rare Bugattis for £92,000. A conservative estimate of their worth today is £1,500,000.

In 1962 the Schlumpfs had owned 35 Bugattis, and, as Fritz put it: "Apart from the Bugattis, I have a beautiful collection of about 70 cars of which half are from 1878 to 1914 and the other half about 1920 to 1940." The staff restoring cars was 15.

By late 1963 the collection had more than doubled and 35 men were on the payroll at Mulhouse while another 15 men were working on the newly acquired Bugattis.

The period between a car's purchase and its arrival filled Fritz with anxiety. After one occasion when a lorry driver stopped for a drink, making him 15 minutes late, Fritz ordered that all cars be shipped by rail.

Unloading was equally fraught. Whatever part of the cars the workers handled, Fritz would intervene, complaining that it

might collapse. "There was no satisfactory way to pick up one of those automobiles in his presence," according to one worker. "You always needed a strong drink after it was over."

Top: *1928 Amilcar CGSS sports two-seater*

Above: *Bugatti Type 101 saloon*

Knowledge of the museum had by now become widespread among enthusiasts and the brothers were constantly besieged by journalists. At one point Fritz, exasperated, announced to Scott Bailey, the publisher of *Automobile Quarterly*, that he was thinking of having all the world's journalists appear at Mulhouse together. He would then wheel each car out for 15 minutes, only on condition that a return visit was never contemplated.

The brothers continued to acquire notable cars. Ellis in Dublin sold them a Silver Ghost chassis, an Isotta, a Franklin and several other cars plus some Harley Davidson motor cycles. A well-known Northern Ireland collector tried in vain to find other buyers for a 'Monza' Alfa and a Bugatti 57S Vanden Plas Coupé, but these also ended up at Mulhouse. As did a Panhard used by

Top: *The original Esders roadster; a rare classic beauty*

Above: *Fritz at the Turkheim race*

French President Poincaré, a Type 40 Bugatti pick-up truck which French explorer Lieutenant Loiseau used to cross the Sahara desert in 1929, and also a small rear-engined Mercedes-Benz saloon.

By now, 40 men were being kept busy in the workrooms. According to one mechanic of the time, Fritz was tireless in supervising the precision work. For example, he would spend endless time going through catalogues of paint colours in order to find just the right tone to match the original colour.

The brothers also had a warehouse of parts including over 100 Bugatti headlamps. Many of the original Bugatti casting patterns had also been acquired from Molsheim.

Having become obsessed with Bugatti by 1965, the brothers were ready to take the next step. They set out to build a Bugatti from scratch that would be better than any other Bugatti.

Car buffs know that Bugatti built only six Royales. The first was Ettore Bugatti's personal car. The others went elsewhere, but contrary to popular myth, none had been ordered by royalty.

The great French couturier, Esders, who virtually invented ready-to-wear had a sports two-seater an elegant advertisement for his firm as it glided through the Grand Boulevards of Paris. Later when Esders sold the car the new owner replaced the coach-work with a new Coupé de Ville.

This car joined another Royale in Bill Harrah's Las Vegas collection. Briggs Cunningham had one in his California museum, and Royale number 4 is in the Ford Museum, Dearborn, Michigan. That left two, the two that are now in the Mulhouse museum.

Under incredible secrecy—they called the project '411'—the Schlumpfs decided to recreate the original Esders car. They got hold of the Bugatti drawings at Molsheim, and a special team went to work.

The chassis and engine took five years, so it was October 1970 before Fritz, his chauffeur Robert Cladin, the chief mechanic on the car Etienne (who was a Bugatti man), and supervisor Jean Joulou, gathered to test the car.

For reasons which are unclear, but may have had to do with his safety, Cladin refused to try the car and the task was passed to Etienne. Once installed behind the wheel, Etienne made an

astonishing confession. He didn't know how to drive. Joulou then replaced him and three hours of satisfactory trials began.

Fritz pronounced himself well satisfied and the chassis was taken, still under a cloak of absolute secrecy, back into the workrooms at Mulhouse. The coach-work was never finished. Royale 'Number 7' was within weeks of completion when the workers took over the factory in 1977. When they entered the workrooms the workers found a retired coach-worker busying himself with this car. He came and went as he pleased and was unaware that the game was up.

Today, there are three enormous, bare, circular platforms in the museum. These were built to display the three Royales.

In May 1965 the Schlumpf brothers, proud of their collection, had some noteworthy visitors. Prince Bertil of Sweden, Prince Louis Napoleon, Prince Metternich, Count Villapadierna, Baron de Graffenreid, Juan Fangio, Pininfarina, Louis Chiron and Artur Keser, formerly public relations chief at Daimler-Benz. On the first day these guests were shown around the cars, which duly impressed them, and were then lavishly entertained by Fritz and his constant companion, Arlette Naas, a hefty quasi-blonde, then in her late 30s. The following day the entire party crossed the German border to the Daimler test track at Underturkheim.

In addition to the Shakespeare Bugattis notable automobiles in the collection at the time of this visit included: a Maserati formerly driven by Farina, a baby Peugeot, a 1898 Clément Panhard, a Type 35B Bugatti and a 1914 Renault Paris taxi.

By now, opening the museum had become an obsession with the Schlumpfs. Fritz spoke of it often. He announced that it would be ". . . in memory of my mother. The collection will go down in posterity under the title of the Collection of Jeanne Schlumpf. I think it's the most beautiful collection in the world, it's unique."

But the collection was also becoming an obsession with the union. Men were constantly being seconded to it from union-defined duties, and items as various as tools, concrete and wood from the forests behind Malmerspach were diverted to Mulhouse. So concerned had the union become that during the general strike of 1968 they put out a list of complaints relating directly to the museum. The brothers ignored it.

Top: *The Esders re-creation*

Centre: *The Schlumpfs' Hotel du Parc*

Above: *Bugatti lamps to burn*

Public entering the "Workers' Museum"

In early September 1969 the Schlumpfs bought the best hotel in Mulhouse, the Hotel du Parc. They decided that if their museum was to attract people from all over the world they might as well provide a package tour and reap the profit. They had the idea of totally redecorating the hotel with automobile motifs.

Where had all the money come from to support this frenetic activity? During and after the war the brothers had done exceptionally well in Malmerspach itself. Then they had expanded by buying factories in 1952, 1956 and 1957 (a facility which they ultimately converted into the museum in 1965). In 1971 they took over another competitor, the Gluck factory in Mulhouse.

By now Fritz's ambitions were enormous. He announced to the workers that virtually "all of the Alsatian woollen industry is now in one pair of hands. This reality of acquiring and possessing and dominating the industry has been my goal for 34 years. It has taken willpower, stubborness, endurance, perseverance, courage, suffering and worry . . . our four factories have been in existence for a total of 365 years . . . 2000 people depend on us for a living and we produce 6,000,000 metres of high quality thread. This is the equivalent of five times the circumference of the world."

While Fritz's words were grandiose, within the year his biggest concerns were immediate and very local. The mills were on strike. The workers' short-term goals were better pay and working conditions but these reflected more basic discontents.

Alsace had always been a backwater. For decades the only question between France and Germany had been whose backwater. Its people were intensely regional. By the beginning of the 1970s the impact of television, the aftermath of the 1968 uprising, and stories from fellow workers on the wealth elsewhere in France, all contributed to the general dissatisfaction with traditional Alsatian life.

And if the central government seemed to shortchange their

province, the Schlumpfs seemed to epitomize all that was worst about the exploitive labour practices in the area. Through the 1940s Fritz and Hans had been regarded as good employers. They paid above-average wages. They were not absentee owners. Quite the opposite. Hans, if anything, was an all-too-present supervisor. In addition workers were assured continuous employment as long as they obeyed the rules.

But by 1971 blind automatic obedience was out of the question. The Socialist Party could not be bought and the Government provided many of the arbitrary benefits the brothers had given in the past. Confrontation was inevitable. The strike which followed was bitter with the workers not only barricading the factories but also occupying the grounds of the villa. When the strike was settled the brothers' interest in the daily operation of the mills became, at best, peripheral.

The riot squad worked overtime

Compensatingly, their interest in the collection became all-important. Here they could see the fruits of their labour. Here they could work closely with skilled craftsmen, as they had when they started up, and here they could find men who shared both their triumphs and their tragedies.

If they found solace in the museum, the outside world seemed increasingly unsympathetic. Precisely how the Schlumpfs accumulated such enormous debts remains in doubt. The total obligation to their creditors is beyond dispute—an enormous eight million francs.

Part of this debacle was beyond their control. Synthetic fabrics were replacing wool, money was harder to borrow, and wages—tied to inflation—were booming. Dismissing the total sales force (which they did) and delegating authority on the basis of loyalty rather than ability did not help. Many able executives left. Others found themselves seconded to working on the museum in Mulhouse.

The size of the enterprise had certain advantages. Exact details are now being sorted out in the courts, but what facts are available suggest that company money was being siphoned off to support the enormous cost of the work on the cars.

In addition, raw materials and semi-finished goods from the other Schlumpf mills were being sold to their factory at Roubaix for conversion to cloth at grossly inflated prices. These paper profits were also apt to be channelled to Mulhouse rather than put back into the firm. Equipment was allowed to become old and unserviceable. Thus, the mills became less efficient and less competitive, just as competitive pressures were increasing.

These alleged financial manipulations were not helped by the brothers' other financial interests, ranging from the still-closed hotel in Mulhouse to property investments. One Fritz kept an eye on but didn't own was an apartment building at 78 Faubourg St. Honoré owned by Fritz's retarded daughter Marielle, now in her 30s, and living there alone. It was simply too much for two reclusive, autocratic men to handle. Under these circumstances the drive to open the museum appears to have become their overwhelming objective.

Any moves to avert financial disaster at the factories was totally subordinated to this end. In April 1976 Fritz announced

The Hotel Trois Rois, Basle;
well-guarded isolation in elegant
surroundings

that the museum would open in May. May came and went. The museum remained closed. Then in early June there was a strong hint that the museum really was about to open. An advertisement appeared in the local newspaper for hostesses, cashiers, ushers, bartenders and cleaning women. The applicants were to be disappointed.

The citizens of Alsace awoke on June 28 to electrifying news. The local court announced that at the request of the brothers, Gluck and Malmerspach works had been put into receivership. Erstein and Roubaix were to follow in July. The following day the brothers issued a statement saying they would relinquish the mills (though not the museum) to any commercial interest who wished to take them over for the symbolic price of one franc.

The workers seized all four factories. The brothers were virtual prisoners in their own house. Even their white 350SEL Mercedes-Benz had been taken. In September an outside consultant was appointed to sort things out. Then on September 10 workers from the various mills demonstrated at the museum.

The situation at Malmerspach deteriorated rapidly. There were fears for the brothers' safety and the sub-prefect from Thann called in riot police. The brothers fled with just two suitcases. They were driven to the station at Mulhouse and boarded a train for Basle.

Later in the year the consultants submitted their report. It said the mills were losing a total of three million francs a month and requested 12 million francs from the government to bail the companies out.

On February 10 1977 a criminal warrant was issued for Fritz's arrest. The main charge was embezzlement. Typically, Hans followed Fritz. His warrant was issued the following day. The consultants announced that, without guaranteed finance, they could not keep the mills open and 1900 workers were sacked.

March also was an eventful month. It began with the workers occupying the museum. It was seized on March 7. During the previous weekend Fritz's daughter had died from a massive heart attack after falling in her bathroom. In one week Fritz had lost his most cherished possessions. The government's final decision against providing finance was made in April and the brothers' possessions, including the museum were ordered to be seized.

On May 12 the unemployed workers of Malmerspach took an unrestored Austin 7 and put it to the torch. Their spokesman, Pierre Schopfer, warned: "Since the attitude has been that there are workers to burn, we have cars to burn. There are 600 more where this one came from."

What will now happen to the museum? For the forseeable future it will be tied up in the courts.

Today, Fritz and Hans are living in well-guarded isolation on the top floor of the elegant Hotel Trois Roi in Basle. Rumour has it that the hotel is theirs. This is impossible to verify. What can be verified are the facts of the recent forced sale of Fritz's personal 350SEL. It was purchased by a middleman for an anonymous Swiss buyer. Given the 96,000-plus kilometres on the clock the price paid was exceptional, nearly twice the going rate. The start of another collection perhaps?

Above: "There are 600 more where this one came from"

Left: Fritz's seized Mercedes 350SEL. The start of another collection?

EARLY DAYS

It is obvious from the Schlumpf collection that the history of motoring, according to Fritz and Hans Schlumpf, is based upon a very special calendar; that of the development of Ettore Bugatti's cars. It was Fritz Schlumpf's dream to possess at least one example of every Bugatti produced. He nearly succeeded.

Bugattis are what you see first, as you enter the museum. Bugattis are what you see last. Scores of Bugattis. Yet among this vast array are many other cars which would be the pride of many a collection. Some Bugatti himself might well have been associated with. Some are rivals providing a contrast to his own cars. Others are a selection from the history of motoring as Bugatti might have known it, especially in his formative years.

Like all true connoisseurs, the Schlumpfs had a wider vision of automotive history than simply the cars produced by Bugatti. There is a substantial selection of early automobiles among the many different models they collected. These ungainly and often bizarre vehicles look somewhat incongruous compared to the sleek machines of later years, particularly to those which represent the heyday of the sporting Bugattis. They do give the Schlumpf collection a definite historical respectability.

Though steam-powered vehicles had enthusiasts—who ensured their survival until the 1920s—they never exerted any major fascination on the Schlumpfs. It was only as conscientious collectors that they made a passing reference to steam, and then only from the very early days when steam power vied with the petrol engine.

The earliest car in the collection is the Jacquot, a small steam-powered cart, that dates from between 1875 and 1878. The vehicle has been described as having a locomotive front end with a horse carriage behind; a French writer once referred to it as a "six seater tonneau brake". The whole venture is supposed to have cost Dr Jacquot some 50,000 gold francs and an endless amount of trouble.

Just beyond the entrance are several steam-powered vehicles and these set the scene for the automobile history to be unfolded. These range from primitive horseless carriages to a splendid Serpollet racing car of the type that competed in the 1903 Paris-Madrid race.

A magnificent black and yellow carriage on ski runners, and a Sicilian peasant's cart are included by the Schlumpfs, reminders of an age that vanished when the motor car arrived. The Jacquot steamer comes next and this aspect of road locomotion ends with relatively sophisticated examples of steam cars. The Ripert, for example, has its saloon body mounted on trestles alongside the chassis, so that the complicated under-chassis workings can be examined.

If the Schlumpfs were only interested in steam's historic perspective Count Albert de Dion was the committed enthusiast. At the age of 20 he had built himself a toy steam engine. In 1883 he enlisted Georges Bouton and his brother-in-law Trépardoux, who ran a small machine shop, and formed de Dion, Bouton et Trépardoux, to build steam-driven road vehicles. They sold 20 tricars before 1899.

In 1893, de Dion came up with a novel idea. He used a

Top: *Dr Jacquot's steam-powered vehicle built in 1875 was little more than a primitive cart. The narrow front track must have made it rather unstable*

Right: *An early steam-powered car with 'vis à vis' seating*

Above: *A Serpollet steam-powered racing car of the type that competed in the 1903 Paris-Madrid race*

Far left: *An elegant horse-drawn carriage set on skis*

Left: *This very early solid-tyred veteran steam car, with independent front suspension, has so far defied total identification*

A 1908 Mercedes four-cylinder with chain-drive

tractor unit as a horse substitute and hooked it up to tow a carriage. The front axle of the carriage was removed so that the whole unit became a semi-trailer rather than a drawbar trailer. Therefore, de Dion can claim to be one of the first producers of a successful articulated vehicle.

However, steam-powered cars were to prove unsatisfactory. As the Schlumpf collection reflects, the end of the 19th century was a time of mushrooming success for the petrol-engined automobile, from firms such as Daimler, Benz and Panhard.

Many of the early vehicles in the collection form part of an illustrated mechanical history of the fortunes—and misfortunes—of various manufacturers. Peugeot and Renault, for example, and Gottlieb Daimler and Karl Benz, the two Germans to whom the whole birth of the motor industry is accredited.

In the case of Daimler and Benz the museum has grouped together early examples of their vehicles. They are displayed in chronological order and show how the two progressed from before the turn of the century until they merged in 1926 to form the great Daimler-Benz AG empire.

Among the collection's Daimler cars (called Mercedes from the turn of the century) is a rare chain-driven model of 1906. Benz illustrates the very beginning of the automobile as we know it today. From 1926 the Mercedes-Benz cars are represented in the collection by an impressive array of large and powerful sporting cars up to the famed 300SL 'Gull Wing' model of 1955. There are also more mundane Mercedes-Benz vehicles: a 170V two-seater tourer, and a rare rear-engined 170H.

Karl Benz produced the first really practical motor car. In 1886 he was granted a German patent for a car which ran on 'Benzine', then sold only in pharmacies. He nearly went bankrupt but by 1888 was producing reasonably successful

petrol-powered four-stroke engines mounted in primitive, solid-tyred, three-wheeled vehicles. Early Benz Victoria and Benz Velo models are displayed in the collection, together with a Benz engine.

A rare 1906 Mercedes six-cylinder with chain-drive

Karl Benz was not a particularly innovative man and he often clung to outdated ideas. By the turn of the century his machines had been surpassed by those of other makers. These incorporated front-mounted vertical engines, in direct opposition to the Benz dictum of rear-mounted horizontal engine, chain or shaft-drive of better design, pneumatic tyres and wheel steering. Nevertheless, by 1896 he had turned out some 181 cars.

While Benz concentrated on complete cars, his rival, Gottlieb Daimler, devoted his time to the perfection of the petrol engine, and to building engines for all purposes. These were installed wherever the opportunity arose, and within a short time taxis, motorboats, fire pumps and airships had Daimler engines.

The early lead taken by German manufacturers was eroded by the end of the century, as emphasis shifted to France. By 1890 both Peugeot and Panhard were established and were building automobiles using Daimler engines made under licence. Eight years later the French motor industry was thriving on an unparalleled scale.

Peugeot and Renault are well represented in the Schlumpf collection. Both have many early examples on show, some like the vast 1912 Peugeot tourer, are exceedingly rare. More popular models include the row of Bébé Peugeots, that vary only in colour. The great French firm Panhard-Levassor has also provided the Schlumpfs with rare pieces, from solid-tyred veterans of the 1890s to majestic Coupé Chauffeur models of the 1908-1910 period.

Before entering the car industry the Peugeot family was

Right: *An imposing 1912 Peugeot tourer*

Below: *A trio of Peugeot Bébés that vary only in colour*

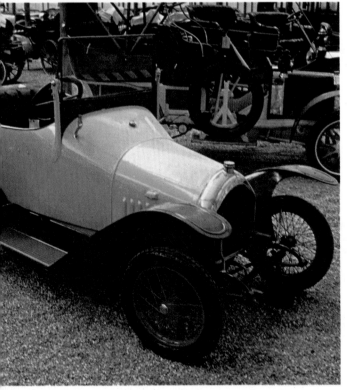

1899 Gladiator with rear-mounted engine

engaged mainly in steel manufacture. They also had a hand in offbeat products: corset stays, crinoline frames, clock and watch springs and coffee and pepper mills. Armand Peugeot was the guiding force in developing the family's car interests. The first cars he manufactured were steam-powered three-wheelers.

Later, Peugeot was approached by Emile Levassor, originally the manufacturer of wood and metal band saws, and the two men collaborated on a design similar in its general lines to Daimler's 'Stahlradwagen'. Their first effort came to nothing, though a prototype built in 1891 was a resounding success. It was sold to a German buyer in Mulhouse (Alsace was then part of Germany) and entered automotive history as the first French car export.

In the next decade Peugeot prospered. Armand, who wanted to concentrate on automobiles, left the family business in 1897 and formed his own company, the Société Anonyme des Automobiles Peugeot. Three years later he was among France's three biggest manufacturers.

The marathon inter-city races of the time were the proving ground for new machines and also the major way of promoting new makes. Much of Peugeot's later success can be attributed to his cars' performances. In the 1894 Paris-Rouen trial (the world's first motoring contest) and in the Paris-Bordeaux-Paris event the following year, Peugeot cars attained average speeds of 11.5mph and 13.4mph respectively. Manufacturers were then quoting 9-12mph as maximum speeds.

Another entry into the fledgling French car industry at the end of the century was René Panhard who, in 1887 with Emile Levassor, obtained the sole rights to build Daimler engines in

France. They produced their first car in 1890. It had a Daimler V-twin cylinder engine placed at the front of a reinforced wooden chassis suspended on fully elliptical springs. The engines were a great success, but the tiller steering was clumsy. This was later rectified and the company scored a great success in 1895 when it introduced both the more powerful Phénix engine and a great innovation—the steering wheel.

Solid-tyred 1892 Panhard-Levassor with wood and metal bodywork, powered by a Daimler engine

Daimler built the first four-cylinder engine for Panhard-Levassor in 1896 and their cars were able to romp through the 1897 Paris-Marseilles-Paris race.

Levassor ran into a stray dog during the Lyon-Avignon stage of the race, his car overturned and he died of his injuries. Although the company name did not change, the cars came to be known simply as Panhards.

By 1900 the typical Panhard had a front-mounted engine, four-speed gearbox and final drive by side-chains. This 'Système Panhard' was copied freely.

Panhards had had unrivalled success in motor racing until 1900 but they were about to be overtaken by the Mors brothers, with their massive 10.1-litre engines.

Speeds were directly proportional to sheer brute power. In 1901, for instance, Panhard cars were mounted with 7.4-litre racing engines that were rated at 40bhp. The 10.1-litre Mors four-cylinder developed 60bhp. Panhard replied with a monster 13.7-litre that gave 80bhp. By 1903 cars like this were setting average speeds of more than 60mph "as fast as an express train."

Panhard-Levassor cars are well represented in the Schlumpf museum. They range from an 1892 solid-tyred veteran powered by Daimler, to one of the last racing cars, a chain-driven 1908 model. The great years of their town carriage are shown by the trio of Coupé Chauffeur saloons of 1908-1909. They are displayed with many of Renault's early production models.

While racing cars were being fitted with bigger and bigger engines, a successful 137cc air-cooled single-cylinder engine was being developed by de Dion. Four years later in 1899 when the first production car fitted with this engine appeared, the cylinder size had risen to 402cc. Cars fitted with these lightweight power units were christened 'voiturettes', the diminutive of *voiture* or car; this became the colloquial name for small cars under 1 litre.

By 1902 de Dion were mounting this engine in the front of their cars, under a Renault-like inverted coal-scuttle bonnet with an under-slung radiator through which the starting handle passed. The engine was a huge success. By 1903 single-cylinder de Dion 'voiturettes' were able to clip along at a respectable 25-30mph. The engine ended up powering more than 140 makes of car, including Peugeot, Delage, Renault and Decauville. Examples from these companies are in the museum.

Illustrating this movement in the French industry is a group of early de Dion cars with veteran Renaults using de Dion engines. It shows how the industry was interwoven in its early days.

It was no surprise that Louis Renault was attracted by de Dion engines. His early light cars had a 1¾hp de Dion single-cylinder

1908 Panhard chain-drive racing car

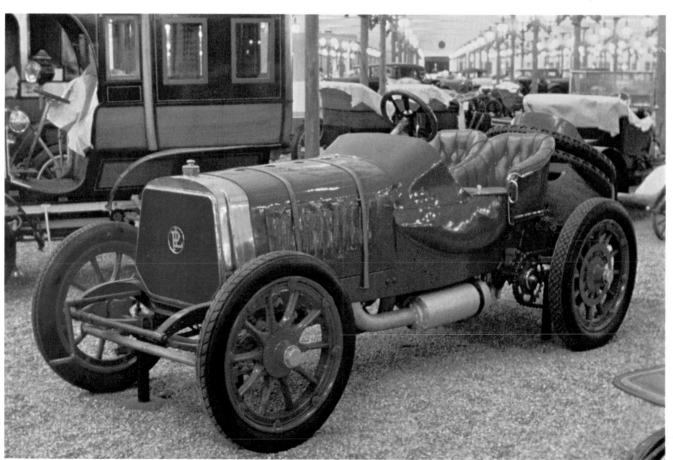

engine at the front of a simple chassis. This car also had a three-speed gearbox, propeller-shaft and differential rear axle. The gearbox was fitted with a direct-drive top gear which Renault patented himself and which others were to use.

A later model with a 500cc water-cooled de Dion won its class in the 1900 Paris-Toulouse-Paris race, setting an average speed of 18.8mph. In 1901 it won the Paris-Bordeaux race (averaging 34.3mph). This near doubling in speed came from doubling the power output to 16hp. Both single and twin-cylinder de Dion engines were being fitted into Renault production models by 1902.

France was now firmly established as the leading nation in the car industry. More than 130 companies competed with each other as comparatively little capital was needed. A manufacturer could make some parts himself and buy others from specialist firms. Britain, France and Germany all had countless suppliers of components such as engines, gearboxes, axles. Labour was cheap and it was possible to make a profit on as few as 100 cars a year usually produced in chassis form. The bodywork was left to specialist coach-builders.

In this entrepreneurial atmosphere it is not surprising that the companies were linked by a web of designers, engineers and drivers. Designers were often hired for a specific machine with no obligations other than the patents they assigned to their temporary employers. Marius Barbarou, for instance, was with *1912 Hispano-Suiza 'Alfonso'*

Adolphe Clément, Karl Benz and de Dietrich, where Bugatti had worked. As a result the cars were often similar in design.

The Schlumpfs seem not to have set out to create a representative collection of veteran cars; but have included many outstanding models giving a good idea of how the industry was entwined in the Franco-German area of Alsace Lorraine.

Spain never figured largely in the early years with the exception of Hispano-Suiza. Its origins lie in the firm of La Cuadra, later renamed Castro after a financial reorganisation. The company still lost money and in 1904, with new backing, it was relaunched as Hispano-Suiza with the Swiss engineer Marc Birkigt in charge of design. The last Castro car became the first Hispano-Suiza. The firm became partly French, and ultimately the French end became an aero engine concern, eventually taking over the Bugatti factory in Alsace.

As if to perpetuate the memory of this sad happening, a number of Hispano-Suiza cars are displayed in the museum, from a 1912 sports model 'Alfonso' to the last of the luxury V-12 saloons of the late 1930s. The 'Alfonso' was named after Alfonso XIII of Spain, an enthusiastic Hispano-Suiza customer who bought 30 of their cars. In 1909 the Queen gave her husband an Hispano two-seater in white with gold lining and golden wire wheels as a birthday present. The King, naturally enough, was pleased to allow his name to be given to the car. It was powered by a 3620cc engine which delivered 64bhp and gave the car a speed of well over 70mph.

Hispano-Suiza were flourishing and established a French assembly plant, a better base from which to create a market for luxury cars. While the sporting 'Alfonso' was a great success, they were aiming for better things. In 1919, they launched the famous H6 model which finally set the seal on their standing in the luxury market. Later examples are included in the Schlumpf collection.

It is, however, the ultimate and highly original works of Ettore Bugatti, which bear his name in the famous elliptical badge, that dominate the museum. In 1899 Ettore Bugatti became an apprentice tester and development driver for the firm of Prinetti and Stucchi of Milan. He seems to have been remarkably free to follow his own inclinations and before he was 17 had successfully modified and raced a tricycle, powered by two de Dion engines. Later, he raced a multi-cylinder quadri-cycle proving he could develop and drive machinery. The same year he also started to design and build a home-made car, even making the foundry patterns himself. Perhaps it was because of personal experience that he later decreed that only simple tools be used in his works. Prinetti and Stucchi were not ready for cars, so Bugatti obtained sponsorship from his father and then from Count Gulinelli. The car which resulted was fairly conventional. It had its engine in the front, the gearbox in the middle and a final drive by side chains. But the engine owed nothing to de Dion. It was a water-cooled, four-cylinder unit of some 3054cc with overhead valves. The four-speed sliding-pinion gearbox was also Bugatti's own creation.

The Italian importer of Benz cars, Guiseppe Ricordi, was a

Above: Veteran Benz Velo with solid tyres and an unusual canopy top supported on a single pole

Left: Steam-powered vehicles like this vied with the petrol-powered Benz of the early days

1912 Lorraine fire engine

Above: *Lorraine-Dietrich omnibus that plied the roads around Malmerspach*

Right: *Row of early bonnets*

family friend and the Bugatti-Gulinelli was displayed on Ricordi's stand at the 1900 Milan exhibition. It was highly praised and although never in production, it came to the attention of Eugène de Dietrich who was making cars at Niederbronn in still-German Alsace. Ettore Bugatti signed an agreement with de Dietrich and moved from Milan to Alsace in 1902.

The first of the de Dietrich Bugatti cars was built in 1903 with a 5.34-litre engine. The cylinders were cast in pairs and encased in aluminium water jackets. Twin gear-driven side camshafts operated overhead valves by pull-rods; cantilever arms attached to the rods pulled the valves down. A similar 30hp version was also produced in the same year. Although Parisian manufacturers were probably unaware of its significance, this marked the beginning of a dynasty.

By 1904 de Dietrich had decided that Niederbronn should stop making cars and production was left to the French branch. Bugatti's two-year contract was over and he joined his friend Emile Mathis, in Strasbourg. Mathis, an agent for both de Dietrich factories, also imported Rochet-Schneider, Panhard, Minerva and Fiat cars. All would have been familiar to Bugatti, and isolated examples of Minerva, Rochet-Schneider and Fiat are at Mulhouse. As already mentioned, Panhards figure prominently. A Lorraine-Dietrich omnibus of about 1912 is of particular local interest. It would have plied the local routes around the Col du Bussang and Malmerspach, where the Schlumpfs founded their empire. A Lorraine fire engine of the same period keeps this bus company, along with Lorraine tourers from 1922-1924.

As this chapter illustrates, the hurly-burly of the dawn of the car industry is well reflected in the collection. By the time that Bugatti set up as a manufacturer in his own right, the car industry was well established—it had suffered its growing pains, and gone up its many 'blind alleys'.

Independent front suspension of early steam car

MIDDLE OF THE ROAD

Most of the cars in the Schlumpf collection fall naturally into categories: Early Days, Bugatti, Sports and Grand Touring. Inevitably this means that some interesting and desirable models were left out. Here is a representative selection of these cars. They are not necessarily exotic or exciting—but they are certainly not to be missed.

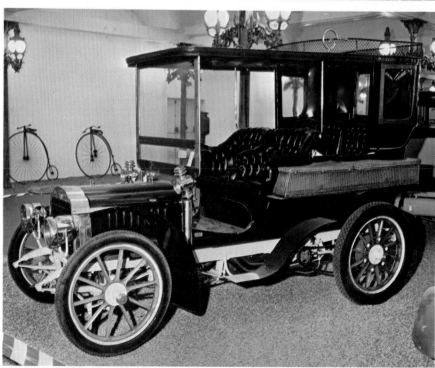

Above: *de Dion Bouton 'Torpedo' four-cylinder*

Right: *Mors Type N; bodywork by J. Rothschild Fils*

Top: *Two Ner-a-car motorcycles, and an ABC motorcycle*

Left: *'Cloverleaf' Citroen 5CV*

Below left: *Austro Daimler, about 1930*

Below: *Ballot 2-litre saloon*

Above: *Daimler Type 38HP,
about 1911*

Right: *Gregoire*

Top: *Tatra V-8 Type 87, about 1938; air-cooled rear engine*

Centre: *Sizaire-Naudin, 1910, one cylinder; with independent front suspension*

Left: *Mercedes-Benz 170H; rear-engined saloon*

BUGATTI

The Mulhouse museum has the largest single collection of Bugattis in the world: nearly 10 percent of the 1600 in existence. The collection was not founded with Bugattis. A Serpollet steamer is thought to be the first car the brothers bought. Yet long before the museum was ever contemplated they owned and raced—in at least one local hill climb—a Type 35T Bugatti.

If there was a reason for their apparent obsession with the *marque* it certainly does not appear to be greed. The fact that the collection is so very valuable (estimates of £10 million may be conservative) is a result, not a cause, of the obsession. It was the Schlumpfs' fanatical pursuit of every Bugatti that inflated the cars' value. Moreover, having cornered the market—and ruined themselves—the brothers did not attempt to realise their assets.

Fritz Schlumpf handled negotiations for the cars in the same bizarre manner with which he dealt with everything else. His behaviour was firmly in the classic eccentric tradition. He would approach owners with offers that many were unable to refuse. Those that did refuse had a new price base on which to value their cars—Bugatti inflation was on its way, fuelled by the Schlumpfs' increased offers to the obstinate.

No sellers were disappointed at the time. And although owners of small collections found the Schlumpfs to be hard bargainers, the brothers were the only people prepared to buy so many cars at once.

Their acquisition of the cars and other items of interest at Molsheim before the Bugatti factory was sold to Hispano-Suiza, was especially significant. They included post-war prototypes which had never come to fruition, and several specimens of work by Bugatti and other designers. There were also unlikely items such as a stock Model-T Ford.

This block purchase was shrewdly conducted: Bugatti was desperate for funds. The brothers knew this and Bugatti's bankers insisted that the £50,000 offer be accepted. The Schlumpfs thus acquired the cars, numerous parts, and the precious foundry patterns for almost all castings for pre-war Bugattis.

The first car in the collection which can truly be called a Bugatti design is the 1904 Hermes Simplex. It is set alongside early Bugattis, on the left of the entrance.

The car was made by Bugatti while working for Emile Mathis in Strasbourg. Though it is properly called a Hermes Simplex, it appeared in at least one British Motor Exhibition bearing a Bugatti label. The *Car Illustrated* report of the 1905 motor show said much was likely to be heard of the car in the racing world: a prophetic understatement.

A new Hermes was built at Graffenstaden. It looked like a de Dietrich with angle corners to the radiator shell. The engine also appeared similar, with oval aluminium water jackets around its two pairs of cylinders. Inside a single camshaft used pull-rods for the overhead inlet valves. Some 60 Hermes designs were built. The model in the collection is a 1904 Hermes Simplex 40HP.

A classic picture of the time shows a 40HP with a mass of notables in or near the car. Ettore Bugatti is at the wheel, surrounded by Fiat's founder, Giovanni Agnelli, Ettore's successful artist brother Rembrandt, Pierre Marchal of Berliet, Fiat driver

Felice Nazzaro, Lancia's founder Vincenzo Lancia, driver Louis Wagner, Cavaliere Scarfiotti, Emile Mathis and Ernest Friderich.

Ernest Friderich, who worked for Mathis and who was then with Bugatti until 1924 as his righthand man recorded much of the early Bugatti days in his memoirs. Friderich was head test driver, salesman, organiser and also a most successful Bugatti racing driver.

He recalls: "It was in one of these cars (Hermes Simplex) that in 1905 I took part as mechanic to 'Le Patron' who was the driver, in the Kaiserpreis at Homburg, and later in the Prince Henry Trials."

Soon after these trials Mathis and Bugatti split up. Mathis continued making cars and finally sold out to Citroen in 1954. The sole Mathis representative of the years following the split-up is a small sporting two-seater of the mid-1920s.

Bugatti now worked as consulting engineer to the Deutz Gas Engine Company, at Cologne, installing himself in a villa near to the car-building works for whom he produced a prototype. This was produced under licence and Bugatti became manager of the car-building department of the Deutz Gas Engine Company. Friderich went to do his military service and returned in time to rejoin Bugatti at Molsheim.

Bugatti resigned from Deutz at the end of 1909 and returned to Alsace. The true Bugatti business started in a garden shed at Molsheim in 1910. The new venture was backed by the Darmstadt Bank, one of whose directors was Senor de Vizcaya. His three sons were later to win fame as Bugatti drivers.

By the beginning of 1911 the Bugatti works were rapidly expanding. Bugatti employed 65 workers and installed himself, Friderich and three others in a separate workshop to experiment. There they assembled a new 7HP which Friderich presented to the Wanderer works at Chemnitz in Saxony, and to Peugeot at Beaulieu. Peugeot bought the licence. This was the original Bébé Bugatti, or model BB, that became the Bébé Peugeot. The Schlumpf collection includes that first famous prototype with its Bugatti radiator. Bugatti evidently liked the idea of producing a car that was smaller than his regular Type 13—but still a car, rather than the primitive cycle-cars of the period.

The BB was designed for mass production rather than to the individual high standards normally associated with Molsheim. Usually produced in open two-seater form, it was a neat machine with a little, low radiator. The engine was a tiny 855cc (55 x 90mm) four-cylinder cast as a monobloc with side valves across the engine—a T-head. The chassis had semi-elliptic leaf springs at the front with the forward ends mounted on very slender dumb-irons (chassis extensions). There were, of course, no front brakes. The rear had reversed quarter-elliptic springs which Bugatti was to use on every subsequent design. The car featured the pear-shaped radiator—destined to become famous even though it subsequently changed into a horse-shoe shape.

Another Bugatti project of the time, and one which was rather out of its design context, was the big 5-litre four-cylinder. An example stands near the little BB. This model was offered in limited quantity in 1912. The car in the collection is virtually

The prototype Bugatti BB baby car,
which became the production Peugeot
Bébé; it had the first of the pear-shaped
radiators seen on all early Bugattis

1904 40HP Hermes Simplex, one of Ettore Bugatti's earliest works

unused. It came in chassis form with the rest of the material from the Bugatti factory in 1963 and a body was built for it.

Ettore Bugatti wrote to a previous owner of one of these cars: "I only built a few cars of this type, which was one of the best models of the period. The first one was built in 1908 and the first sale was in 1912. The car which you have was delivered on September 18, 1913, to my late regretted friend Roland Garros, the airman of whom you have doubtless heard . . .

"It will perhaps interest you to know that the valve control design as used on this car is the one adopted by Messrs. Rolls-Royce for their aeroplane engines."

The *raison d'être* for this model has never really been properly established. The 1908 date given by Bugatti seems to refer to a prototype of similar size driven in competition by Bugatti. It may well have been based on Deutz parts.

Bugatti's 1910 catalogue contains all the Type 13 model information. It also shows some of the designs of his past, among which—dated 1910—is a Prince Henry with wooden spoked wheels whereas the final 5-litre cars all had wire wheels. The chassis design suggests it was conceived in 1908 because it still used chain-drive—a feature not used by Bugatti thereafter. After Roland Garros was killed in action in 1915 the 5-litre was always known as the 'Garros Type'.

M. Hylle, a great friend of Ettore, took part in the Prince Henry Trials with Friderich as his riding-mechanic in one of these cars. This event through Germany and Alsace passed through Molsheim where Madame Bugatti set up a buffet for competitors at the gates of the Bugatti estate. Friderich recalls the joy of being able to pull up there: "We enjoyed an excellent glass of champagne and splendid sandwiches. At the end of the race we were declared the winner on points . . ."

The Roland Garros car has been in England for many years. With it is a collection of spare parts which, when recently assembled, were found to comprise almost a complete car. So now there are three in existence, the 'spares' having been assembled into a complete and running car fitted with a replica of a contemporary racing body.

Bugatti's type numbers may seem a little bewildering, but they were usually chronological and many people have attempted to

Unused Bugatti 'Garros Type' acquired from the Molsheim factory

draw up a definitive list. There is no record at the Molsheim factory of a type number for this 5-litre car. The French historian Serge Pozzoli has suggested Type 16, but this is not logical since Types 15 and 17 were allocated in 1911.

During the First World War Bugatti concentrated most of his efforts on aero engines. They do not seem to have been as successful as those of his cars. The collection contains two 16-cylinder units, and one of the eight-cylinder units on which they were based. The eight-cylinder was of classic Bugatti line with the single overhead camshaft driven at the rear of the engine. Drive for the magneto and water pump came off skew gears. These were positioned as on existing Bugatti engines but the oil pump was driven off the middle of the crankshaft.

This engine was licensed to both Diatto in Turin and Delaunay-Belleville in St. Denis, outside Paris. Neither produced it in great numbers although French-made versions went to America where Duesenberg produced the 16-cylinder. Later a straight-eight Diatto was to sire the Maserati empire.

Bugatti's 16-cylinder aero engine design was in effect a pair of eights with crankshafts geared to a central shaft. This drove a propeller shaft mounted between the two banks. It was extremely compact for its time and represented 2lb weight per horsepower. Sixty years later the modern Grand Prix engine is about ¾lb per horsepower.

The American in charge of development of the H16 at the Duesenberg Motor Company—later the makers of some grand cars in the same mould as Bugatti's Royales—was Charles B. King. The engine was called a Bugatti-King, and King embarked on a series of improvements. Bugatti viewed these with hearty disapproval although he was later to adopt some.

Apart from a number of detail modifications, like rounded camcovers instead of rectangular ones, for easier casting, the Americans enlarged on the basic design.

They were impressed by the engine's smoothness, its compactness with a better power-to-weight ratio than either Rolls-Royce or Liberty, and clever use of gearing which allowed firing a gun through the propeller. The continuous rating of the 24.3-litre engine was 420bhp at 1996rpm rising to a maximum of 500bhp at 2300rpm.

Above: *Bugatti-King H16 aero engine, 1918*

Right: *Very pretty 1914 three-seater long wheelbase Type 13 Bugatti. The four-cylinder engine is the touring eight-valve version*

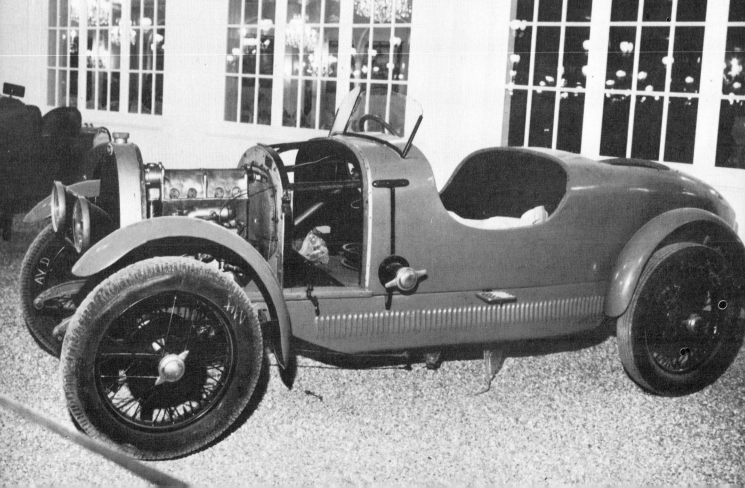

Despite their enthusiasm, the engine never went into full production. Armistice was signed a few days after it passed its 50-hour endurance test. Although orders had been placed for 2000 engines four months earlier, only 40 were ever produced.

By 1919 Bugatti was back into car production, perfecting the Type 13 four-cylinder. After the war Alsace became part of France. The Bugatti, a car with an Italian name and which had originated in German territory, was now to race in French national blue.

When work resumed at the Molsheim factory, Bugatti concentrated on the 16-valve four-cylinder engine for standard production. This was installed in the road-going Types 22 and 23, while the short-chassis version was the Type 13, to be used for competition. The line of early four-cylinder Bugattis just inside the museum door includes a pair of Type 13 cars, known as 'Brescia'. The name was given after the race in Brescia, Northern Italy, in September 1921 in which Type 13 cars finished in the first four places.

To prepare for this race Bugatti worked on installing ball or roller bearings for crankshaft and big-ends on his engines. He settled for a plain front bearing, with ball-bearings in the centre and at the end of the split crankshaft. The big-ends used split roller cages, thus avoiding the usual practice of splitting the whole crankshaft. With the capacity limit now 1½ litres the Bugattis had a bore of 68mm to give 1453cc and around 40bhp.

At Brescia opposition from the local makes was minimal. The race was over 20 laps of a triangular 10.7 mile circuit and although a local car took the lead briefly, before retiring, the Bugattis waltzed home. Friderich, de Vizcaya, Baccoli and a new driver, Pierre Marco, who was to remain with Bugatti to the final days of the company, took the first four places at nearly 72mph. This was the fastest 1½-litre light car race of the time.

The name 'Brescia' applied only to the short wheelbase Type 13; the Types 22 and 23 were called 'Brescia modifie'. Roller bearings were used almost throughout on the factory 'Brescias'; normal ones had roller mains and plain big-ends after mid-1923.

Bugatti had a phobia against pressure lubrication even though the Americans claimed to have developed a successful system following disasters on the wartime aero engines—caused, they said, by the primitive lubrication system. Certainly, the system used on the roller-crank 'Brescias' was a remarkable demonstration of how to avoid the sensible alternative.

The main bearings were lubricated by jets, but for the bronze and later white metal big-ends the crankshaft webs had pockets machined into the crank webs, into which oil squirted on each revolution. Later the crank webs were made circular and oil was squirted sideways into grooves which connected to the big-end journals. This was adequate for touring but marginal for racing.

Four-wheel brakes were coming into vogue and by 1925 all Bugattis had them. They appeared first on the Type 28 chassis that was shown in London and Paris in 1921. The car was purely a prototype as regards the eight-cylinder engine and never entered production. The nearest to it was the Type 44 six years later. The show chassis remained at Molsheim and was one of

Top: *Built-up replica of a 'Brescia' Type 13 Bugatti*

Left: *Roadster 'Brescia' Type 23 Bugatti on the long wheelbase chassis*

Fritz's 'catches'. It now carries a recently made open four-seater bodywork, which hides many of the interesting features.

The chassis was a fairly normal channel section frame with the usual Bugatti springing: semi-elliptic leaf springs at the front and reversed quarter-elliptics at the rear. At the front end the drag link and track rod consisted of twin parallel tubes. Road shocks to the driver were minimized by a fabric coupling from the worm and sector steering box. The steering wheel, which had only two spokes, could be adjusted for reach; but this has gone with the passage of time and is replaced by a normal Bugatti four-spoke wheel. The four-wheel brakes were intended to be hydraulic but were such a failure that Bugatti reverted to cable operation until 1938.

The dimensions of the Type 28 followed those of the later 'Brescias' with 69 x 100mm giving 2991cc. Nine plain bearings were used for the crankshaft inside the crankcase; another was contained in a separate casting behind clutch and flywheel. The big-ends were also plain bearings and lubrication was said, at the time, to be full pressure throughout. This is unlikely in view of subsequent designs. The engine had two blocks of four cylinders, but the vertical shaft driving the camshaft came up between the blocks, with magneto and water pump on opposite sides driven by skew gears. At the top of the vertical shaft the bevel gear had two sets of teeth for two gears on the camshaft. The gearing was fractionally different on one set which was connected to the camshaft via a friction clutch. Thus there was always a friction brake taking up any slack in the camshaft drive

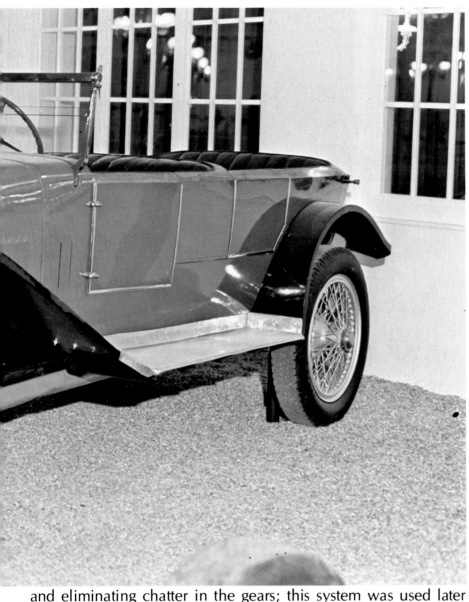

The 1921 prototype of the Bugatti Type 28, which never went into production, has been recently bodied with this open four-seater

and eliminating chatter in the gears; this system was used later on the Royale Type 41. As with the 'Garros', there were three valves per cylinder—two inlet and one exhaust—operated via finger followers between cam and valve.

With individual supply of combustible mixture through special Bugatti carburettors to each block of four cylinders, the engine was said to produce 90bhp at 3400rpm. It was a fine-looking engine, with that classic square architecture which featured from then on. There was no gearbox between engine and rear axle as the two-speed mechanism was buried in the rear axle—at the doubtless unappreciated expense of considerable increase in unsprung weight. This layout was used on numerous later Bugatti models, though with a third speed added, as in the Types 41, 46 and 50.

The Type 28 was obviously designed to be a luxury car, as contemporary coach-builders now produce 'dream' cars at motor shows to evoke publicity. Presumably there was little response as Bugatti shelved the idea.

The eight-cylinder Bugatti form went into production as the 2-litre Type 30. It was more simplified than the Type 28, and inspired by the touring four-cylinder Types 22 and 23. The Type 38 was the next touring car; the intervening models were sports and racing cars. The Type 38 used a virtually identical engine to the Type 30 except for a crankcase to sump joint slightly raised to ease construction with the ball-race centre main bearing.

A new gearbox straddled the frame which would further have increased the chassis stiffness. The gear lever was now central instead of on the right. Increasing frame stiffness was probably desirable as the chassis of the Type 38 is slightly longer than that of the Type 30.

Since the Type 38 was produced between 1926 and 1927, when the Bugatti racing department was developing the super-charger for the Type 35 Grand Prix cars, this power-boosting instrument was also available on the Type 38. It then became the Type 38A.

After sorties into streamlining with the Indianapolis cars and the 'tank' Type 32, Bugatti reverted to producing a conventional-looking racing car. This was the famous Type 35, with a flat horse-shoe radiator and neat body tapering to the pointed tail that was *de rigueur* for racing cars of the period.

In an obituary, a fellow-countryman wrote of Bugatti: "He was pure artist; his only scientific knowledge resulted from experience which increased with the years, and a natural mechanical ability aided by a gift of observation. He did not believe in calculations, formulae or principles. He joked about pages of mathematical figures and about integration signs which he called violin holes. He happily had the wisdom to surround himself with talented engineers whom he paid generously, but demanded from them total anonymity." This is evidenced by the multitude of patents in the name of 'E. Bugatti'.

Lessons had quite obviously been learned by the time the Type 35 appeared. In the straight-eight 2-litre engine which followed the general lines of the Type 30, that car's lubrication problems had been overcome: a full roller-bearing layout was used for main bearings as well as big-ends. The drive for the single overhead camshaft followed normal Bugatti practice; a vertical shaft driven by bevel gears from the front of the engine, with a cross-shaft turning the water pump and a worm and roller drive for the oil pump. Three valves per cylinder were used; each had its own cam, with a finger follower operating on the end of the valve.

Bugatti's gearboxes have always been exceptionally neat; his insistence on simple machining, and therefore greater accuracy, dictated the use of square shafts for the sliding pinions rather than the approved method of machined splines. The box was separated from the engine by a short shaft between clutch and gearbox and mounted on tubular cross-members.

Gearchange was by a slender lever poking through the side of the cockpit, for use by the right hand (all Bugattis being righthand drive) and was delightfully precise. The suspension was conventional Bugatti with half-elliptic leaf springs at the front and reversed quarter-elliptics at the rear. The front axle confounded the experts, having a dropped-centre hollow axle through which the leaf springs passed.

The Type 35's most notable feature was its cast aluminium wheels with integral brake drums. These were made in two parts, with inner and outer rows of the large flat spokes backed by a finned drum with a cast-iron liner. The outer part was the detachable rim bolted on to the main casting by 24 countersunk set-screws, to be undone with a screwdriver. Later the heads had a machined square for a special key!

Ettore Bugatti stands behind one of his first Type 35 Grand Prix cars at the 'weighing-in' before the 1924 French Grand Prix at Lyon

The Type 35, and its derivatives, was one of the most attractive and functional designs to appear from Molsheim. It scored racing victories throughout the world. No wonder there is a complete stand devoted to examples of this most classic of all racing Bugattis in Mulhouse.

Despite the Type 35's many virtues and subsequent successes, the first event in which it appeared, the 1924 French Grand Prix at Lyon was a disaster. Bugatti had asked Dunlop to build tyres of special size for his new wheels. In the race there was constant trouble. Various reasons have been given for the faults. Bugatti blamed incorrect vulcanisation; others incorrect design of the wheel rim. The fact is that a month later the wheels performed perfectly with conventional beaded edge tyres of the period at San Sebastian.

Whatever the reason, the basic wheel design was retained on Grand Prix cars and also used on the road-going Types 43 and 55, although later wheel designs had stiffening ribs cast into the back of the spoke blades.

The performance of Bugatti cars in Grand Prix is covered elsewhere, but it is their performance in the free-for-all Targa Florio in Sicily that is really telling. From 1925 to 1929 Bugatti achieved great success in this twisting, turning, climbing race with his Grand Prix cars.

In 1925 Costantini, the Italian who was later to manage Bugatti's team, won from two Peugeots. He won again in 1926 driving a Type 35T, with two more Bugattis following him home. In 1927 Bugatti cars took the first two places and in 1928 a Bugatti beat Campari's Alfa Romeo, with four more Bugattis following. In 1929 Bugattis again took first and second places.

The Targa Florio was ostensibly a sports car race and thus outside Grand Prix regulations, though some of the cars raced in it were virtual Grand Prix cars. When the Grand Prix rules changed to 1½ litres for 1926, Bugatti used the supercharger to gain more power. Before competing in a 1½-litre Grand Prix he experimented in small events in Alsace, with 1100cc versions of his 2-litre engine for the 'voiturette' class. The cars had streamlined cowlings around the classic horse-shoe radiator and used quarter-elliptic front springs and a straight axle beam. These cars were the Type 36 with engine dimensions of 51.3 x 66mm.

The next development of the Grand Prix Type 35 was the Type 39. It had a 1½-litre supercharged engine and differed outwardly principally in its larger radiator.

After the 1925 Targa Florio victory an enlarged version of the 35 with 2262cc capacity was named the 35T, and when this was supercharged the following year it became the Type 35B—the mainstay of racing victories up to 1931. There was also a Type 35A, known in the factory as the 'Course Imitation' or 'fake-racer', which was derived in response to customer requests. It used the Type 35 chassis, and the engine from the touring Type 38, with its three-bearing crankshaft and plain big-ends. The car went well, but was just a street version of the real thing. The French nicknamed it 'Tecla'.

Without a close inspection it is difficult to tell these various cars apart. The supercharged versions normally have a hole in

Above: *Ernest Friderich in a 'tank' during the 1923 Grand Prix at Tours*

Right: *The bizarre Bugatti Type 32 'tank' Grand Prix car that raced at Tours in 1923. The short wheelbase is emphasised in this side view, as is the falling-away front and rear of the body*

Right: *The supercharged 2.3-litre Type 35B, with its shapely radiator now a horse-shoe and cast-aluminium wheels, is the classic Grand Prix Bugatti*

Far right: *Mother and two sons; the Type 35T Bugatti near the museum entrance, with the two electrically driven Type 52 scale models*

94

Above: *Type 35 Bugatti, 2-litre, eight-cylinder*

Right: *Type 37 Bugatti, 1½-litre, four-cylinder*

the righthand side of the bonnet, high up, as an outlet for the blower relief valve.

On the dedication stand to Maman Schlumpf, just inside the door of the museum, is a beautiful Type 35T equipped for use on the roads. It has a bulb horn, spare wheels and number plates. This is the car the brothers used in the Ballon d'Alsace hill climb.

Among the great array of blue Grand Prix Bugattis are some of the smaller and less powerful Type 37 models. The sophistication of the eight-cylinder range had made the cars expensive for owners who previously bought 'Brescias', so Bugatti introduced the four-cylinder version of the Grand Prix car, with a touring derivative as well. The pointed-tail Grand Prix models were the Type 37 or 37A (supercharged) and the touring version was the Type 40, built on a shortened Type 38 chassis.

The Type 37 was loosely based on half of a 3-litre Type 28 engine, with the fixed-head block using 69 x 100mm—1496cc dimensions. The familiar vertical shaft drove the overhead camshaft and lubrication was provided by a worm drive on the nose of the crankshaft. As in the Type 35 engine bearers came off the bottom of the crankcase, which formed the sump, with 20 aluminium cooling tubes running through it.

In normal trim with a single Solex carburettor the Type 37 gave around 60bhp at 4500rpm. With a supercharger blowing at 7½psi, the output was near to 85bhp—enough to give the 37A in its Type 35 body and chassis a top speed of over 100mph, against the 85-90mph of Type 37.

In theory the Type 37 can be distinguished by its wire wheels *Type 35 Bugatti, 2-litre, eight-cylinder*
against the aluminium of Type 35, but the exotic Grand Prix
wheels and hubs could easily be fitted. On both Type 37
versions the radiator is more like the small slender one on the
original Lyon Type 35. It had the Grand Prix chassis beneath it
and was an excellent little road-cum-competition car, reliable
and easy to maintain. However only 290 examples were made
against 340 of the combined Types 35 and 39.

The touring derivative of the Type 37 was the Type 40 which
used a less highly tuned and more economical engine giving
around 40bhp. In saloon and coupé form it made an excellent
town car. The standard bodywork for this model, built at
Molsheim, was an open four-seater with a pointed tail. In 1929 it
sold for £365, against £725 for the Type 37A, or £200 less
without the supercharger. There was a similar supercharger levy
on the Type 35 range, with the 35B costing £1475.

With the Type 40 a certain amount of sophistication was
introduced. A dynamo was driven off the front of the crankshaft
and protruded through the bottom of the radiator, and a starter
was carried on the crankcase.

Among the Type 40 models at Mulhouse are four-door
saloons, an open four-seater, an exotic 'razor-edged' coupé with
basketwork finish on the side panels, and the standard two-seater
tourer with dickey (rumble) seats. With this group is what
appears to be a crude pick-up truck—in fact a Type 40 'Sahara'.

In 1927 Lieutenant Frederic Loiseau had the idea of crossing

Group of Type 40 Bugattis with a staid four-seater saloon in the foreground, alongside the 'Sahara'. Behind is the rare Type 40A roadster (right)

the Sahara by car and asked Bugatti to supply suitable cars. Bugatti offered to build six suitably modified. These had a Type 40 chassis and wooden bodies with enormous 225-litre containers for petrol. He also agreed to supply the necessary tools, spares and the Dunlop tyres for such an expedition. The cars had no mudguards or windscreens *('visibilite totale')*, straight-through exhausts, and a simple system of recuperation for the cooling system in case of boiling. Ettore Bugatti told Lieutenant Loiseau he would guarantee these cars for 15,000km off the road, but added: "Naturally, you must not fall into holes of more than one metre depth. Up to one metre, O.K."

The 'raid' was carried out in 1929 with total success: the Type 40 covered 14,000km over the sand and rocks of French Equatorial Africa and the Sahara. The remaining example of these rugged little cars rested at Molsheim until bought by John Shakespeare who sold it to Schlumpf. It now stands fiercely proud in its blue wooden bodywork.

With his Grand Prix, sports and touring cars a great success Bugatti wanted to build a really fast tourer, a 'gran turismo' or 'grand sport'. This project appeared in 1927 as the Type 43. It

Above: *The Type 40 Bugatti 'Sahara'
used by Lieutenant Loiseau for his
14,000km African journey*

Left: *Elegant town car, a 'razor edge'
coupé with basketwork side panels on a
Type 40 Bugatti chassis*

was in effect a Grand Prix car with room for the family. Since the
supercharged Type 35B was eminently suitable, it was the basis.
The engine was slightly detuned and lowered into a new waisted
frame, using axles and other chassis parts from the previous
year's Type 38 tourer. Type 35B cast-alloy wheels with the stiffer
spokes were used, and the whole lot was clothed in a four-seater
pointed-tail tourer body, louvred undertray and all. This gave
birth to the Grand Sport. With spare wheel strapped to the
doorless, driver's side it looked what it was—the family man's
racer. It sold for £1200 in England in 1929—£95 less than a
4½-litre Vanden Plas Bentley—and gave 110mph potential in a
car that could still start in top gear and be driven to the shops.
Even by today's standards it is an exhilaratingly quick car to
drive, capable of reaching 90mph in around 30 seconds.

Most of the Type 43s used the works Grand Sport body, but
some were fitted with special coach-work to customers'
requirements by outside firms—in the form of more sporting
two-seaters or even coupés. The factory itself produced a
two-seater car with dickey (rumble) seat, and a transverse
compartment for golf clubs. It was known as the Type 43A.

Post-war experimental Bugatti Type 73 saloon of 1947; it never went into production

Without question the normal two-four seater Grand Sport was the Type 43 to own. In the museum the display devoted to Bugattis of this period includes the most delectable trio in echelon, all in typical Bugatti blue. Five more examples surround them: a drophead coupé, another Grand Sport, a special bodied two-seater, and two 'touring' roadsters. Away in a corner among some later Bugattis is a complete chassis.

The idea of turning a successful Grand Prix car into a usable road-going sports or touring car, came up again in 1932, when Ettore's growing son Jean was involved. This was the Type 55 which was evolved from the twin-cam Type 51 Grand Prix car.

It was Ettore's dream that one day he would produce the ultimate road car, as opposed to cars used exclusively for racing or sporting events. The answer he came up with was his 1926 Bugatti Royale, the 13-litre leviathan that surpassed all others in grandeur. The Royale was originally conceived before the First World War, but Bugatti was then barely past the first rung of the automotive ladder. However, he sought perfection. In 1913 he wrote to his friend Dr. Espanet, and told him he had on the drawing board a car with a 100mm cylinder bore dimension that would be larger than a Rolls-Royce but lighter, and would achieve 100mph in perfect silence.

The outside world was let into the Royale secret in mid-1926, with the prototype apparently nearly completed. The engine in this first car was said to be of 125 x 150mm—14,726cc. But in production these dimensions were reduced to 125 x 130mm— 12,763cc. Such an engine is massive beyond belief. All the more usual Bugatti design features were used—on a gigantic scale. The front axle was similar to the Type 35 with the springs passing through it: reversed quarter-elliptic springs supported the massive rear axle, though there were supplementary springs ahead of the axle. The horse-shoe radiator shape was retained and the engine was of the classic square-cut exterior. The engine construction was extremely complex. It had to be completely removed even for comparatively simple maintenance operations. All this was in pursuit of the ultimate in rigidity, silence and long life. Bugatti did not anticipate that a Royale would require any maintenance or overhaul work for at least ten years!

With more than 4½ feet of engine to be hidden, and a wheelbase of 14½ feet to be suitably clad, the coach-builders faced a challenge. The resultant 2½ tons, or more, would also require some stopping from 100mph. The problem could well have provoked some great innovation. But no. Brakes followed the normal four-wheel braking system of most Bugattis: cables and compensating gear.

The wheels were indeed special, scaled up in size like everything else so that the car did not look particularly large from a distance. They were made in cast alloy and had the most superb curved vanes acting as blades to draw air into the brakes or extract it from them, depending which side you were looking at. The three-speed gearbox was contained within the rear axle, and with a gearing of about 40mph per 1000rpm and an engine that would be capable of 2500rpm, the Royale had a good chance of achieving Bugatti's aim of 100mph in silence.

Six chassis were constructed over seven years—hardly a best seller. Even so the Royale has put the name of Bugatti on a special pedestal among car builders.

The first car, which Bugatti kept himself, was rebodied many times—as were two of the others. Altogether there were 11 variations on the theme.

The first Royale with chassis number 41100 (Type 41, number 100—100 always looks more impressive than one) started life as a vast tourer with a Packard-style body. It then had a small coupé body followed by two versions of saloon bodies and ended up with the Coupé de Ville. After the death of 'Le Patron', the car was kept at the Bugatti château until the Schlumpfs bought it.

The Type 38, a 2-litre eight-cylinder with a variety of body styles was one of the early touring Bugattis

The second Royale was built as a two-seater with bodywork designed by Jean Bugatti, for Armand Esders, couturier and king of 'ready-to-wear' clothes in the late 1920s. This was essentially a Bois de Boulogne promenade car, utterly selfish in its use of road space. The ultimate 'cad's car'. Esders did not want to drive at night—perhaps because no one would see the car—so no lamps were fitted. This lovely roadster with a 'hoop' line—the front wings swept down in a graceful curve to short running boards, then swept up in a similar curve in the rear wing—also had a grey-green moulding in subtle contrast.

During the Depression Esders was forced to sell and the new owner ordered Henri Binder's firm to create a Coupé de Ville similar to that of Bugatti's own car. The car was hidden in the Paris sewers during the war and bought by an English owner. It is now in the Harrah Museum, Reno, Nevada.

Dr Joseph Fuchs ordered chassis 41121 and the bodybuilders Weinburger of Munich built him a Cabriolet body. The upholstery was of Hungarian pigskin; the bodywork was subdued, in black with discreet yellow mouldings; the running boards were white moulded rubber. It cost £7500 even then. After a sojourn in the Far East, the car found its way to America where it eventually languished in a junk yard. It was rescued by Charles Chayne of General Motors and is in the Ford Museum, Dearborn, Michigan.

Some seven years after the introduction of the Royale, chassis number 41131 was bought by the Englishman, Captain C.W. Foster, and given a limousine body by Park Ward. After the war it went to America and eventually returned to France when the Schlumpfs acquired the Shakespeare collection of Bugattis.

The remaining two Royales were both used by the Bugatti family. Number 41141 was fitted with a two-door coupé body by Kellner of Paris and was offered, unsuccessfully, for sale at £6500 at the Paris Motor Show. It was later used by Ettore's daughter L'Ebe, until she sold it to Briggs Cunningham who keeps it in his collection at Costa Mesa, Los Angeles.

The final Royale in the production run, if it could be called that, was, curiously, 41150. This also stayed with the Bugatti family. It was fitted with a Cabriolet-like four-door body in black and ivory, described as a 'Berline de Voyage'—touring saloon. This is also in the Harrah Museum.

That might reasonably be thought to be the end of the Royale

Above: *Ettore Bugatti's personal Royale was one of the most elegant cars of all time. This chassis, number 41100, carried a variety of body styles before this Sedanca de Ville was evolved*

Right: *The Park Ward body on Captain C. W. Foster's Bugatti Royale, chassis 41131, was large and conservative*

Far right: *The Royale engine was as imposing as some of the bodywork. This example is actually a railcar engine*

The experimental steam engine intended for the French State Railways is the centrepiece of the museum's Bugatti engine display. It is flanked on each side by an H16 aero engine; in front is a Royale road wheel. On the far left is a railcar engine and, on the far right, a very early eight-cylinder car engine

line. But that reckons without the determination and enthusiasm of the Schlumpf brothers. Obvious admirers of the Esders two-seater in its original form, they spent more than five years building a replica, a 41111 Mark 2.

The chassis frame was made in nearby Belfort and rivetted up in Malmerspach. With sundry patterns from Molsheim and a spare railcar engine, they had a good basis for a new Royale. It was nearing completion when the workers seized control. There the matter stopped.

A problem such as lack of buyers did not deter Bugatti from making use of his Royale engines. He promptly employed them in railcars—'buses on rails' with or without trailers. The first went into service on the Paris-Deauville route, cruising at 70mph with its four engines. Jean Bugatti later drove one at an average of 90mph from Paris to Strasbourg.

The four engines were centrally mounted and drove bogie wheels through hydraulic clutches and propeller shafts; steel wheels and rims had a rubber interlayer and the bogies were fully sprung, so the ride must have been remarkably good. Some 79 units were in service on the French National Railways, the largest carrying 144 passengers. The last went out of service as late as 1958, so spare engines still abound. Many collectors have examples and three are in the Mulhouse museum.

Among the many other engine exhibits is a huge steam engine. This was another Bugatti project for the French Railways. Assisted by his technical director, Noel Domboy, Bugatti designed the prototype unit intending to provide the state railway with a 1000 horsepower tractor-unit, and the PLM with a double tractor-unit of 2000 horsepower. War stopped work.

Inevitably the engine was a straight-eight. The nine-bearing roller crankshaft was carried on the base of the block and the head carried twin overhead camshafts with progressive profile lobes that allowed the timing to be changed as the cams were moved axially. It was designed to run at 700psi and first ran in 1934-1935 using steam from the Molsheim factory boiler. Many tales have been told of those early experiments, and the comedy

of coupling this vast stationary engine to the works heating system. The steam engine, acquired by the Schlumpfs from the Molsheim works, is the centrepiece of a collection of Bugatti engines. Ettore's interest in steam engines dates back to the early 1920s when he experimented with a Stanley steam car—fitting it with a giant boiler which made the car impractical by obscuring the windscreen.

As is often the case, the next type number is totally unrelated to the previous ones. The Type 44 was Bugatti's first really refined production touring car. It had a 3-litre engine with the 'Brescia' dimensions of 69 x 100 mm, and was naturally a straight-eight. Many of its design features came from the shelved Type 28, while the chassis was the same length as the Type 38. Transmission, brakes and axles were as on the Type 43, but wire wheels replaced cast-aluminium, and were often covered by discs which suited the styles of bodywork. It was a refined Bugatti and was intended for the more wealthy man-in-the-street, but not the absurdly rich. It was obviously well received: 1095 were made.

The Type 49, thought by many people to be the nicest and most practical of the Molsheim tourers, was a logical development of the 44. In most respects it was a Type 44 but the few changes made an important difference. The engine had a bigger bore at 72mm, raising the capacity to 3.3 litres with an improvement in low-speed torque rather than ultimate power—all-important in a good touring car. A further refinement was a cooling fan driven from the front of the camshaft, and there were 16 sparking plugs for more impressive ignition. The wheels set it apart. Bugatti seldom conformed to conventional wheels for long and the Type 49 followed the Royale style, with small turbofinning cast in aluminium.

During this period France, and the rest of the world, were climbing out of the Depression and the coach-work, though much in evidence on the Type 49 chassis was far more practical than the far-out exotica of the roaring Twenties.

Molsheim made many bodies. The coach-work department

Bugatti Type 49 coupé

was presided over by young Jean Bugatti who had a flair for such work. He drew full-size elevations and plan views of new styles which were given to the frame-makers. Most of these bodies were aluminium panels on ash frames.

These most worthy of all touring Bugattis proliferated. They showed no specific trends in coach-work, so the 13 examples in the collection vary from sober limousines, through close-coupled saloons to staid drophead coupés.

Bugatti's 'mini-Royale'—the Type 46—was rather more successful in terms of numbers than the Royales. It sold around 400 models. It did not begin to approach the Royale in size but attracted some superbly styled coach-work from Jean Bugatti and others. In 1931 the model cost £975, and another £200 for the supercharged version which made it a 46S. It was 32 inches less in wheelbase and 18 inches less in length; the engine was reduced from 12.8 litres to 5.3 litres.

There were various body styles including an exotic-looking two-door, four-seater coupé with a very sloping windscreen, and four-door four-light saloons with rear trunk covered in fabric. There were saloons, sports two-seaters and two-seater tourers. Most of these styles are shown among the eight examples gathered in the incredible Mulhouse collection.

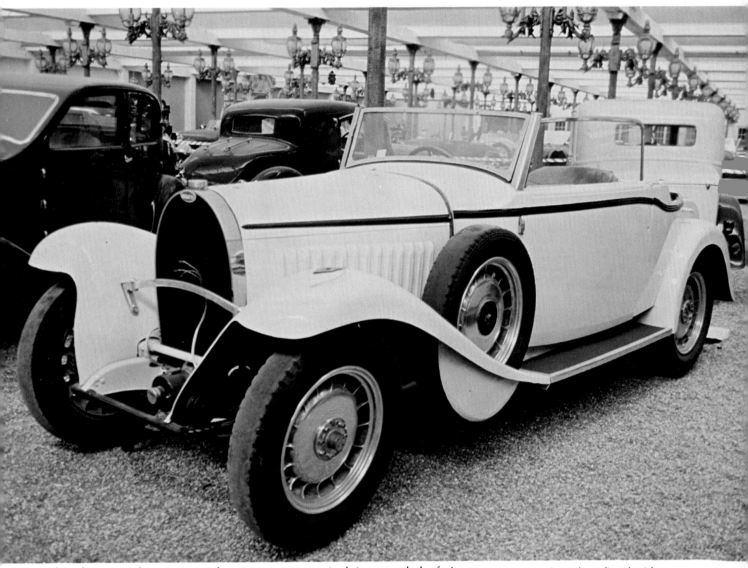

Type 44 Bugatti roadster fitted with a later Type 49 3.3-litre engine

Like the Royale engine, the Type 46 carried its crankshaft in nine main bearings at the base of the block. The drive to the usual single overhead camshaft and three valves per cylinder was by a vertical shaft at the front. Four forged engine bearers were bolted direct to the block, their outer ends in rubber cups to isolate vibrations. Between the crankshaft and flywheel was a rubber shock absorber. From the clutch the propeller shaft disappeared toward the back axle in which the three-speed gearbox is housed.

In unsupercharged form most of the Type 46 cars were capable of 90mph, and probably felt safer than the Royale while doing that speed over normal roads. The Type 46 pleased Bugatti and was also a favourite with racing drivers such as Jules Goux and Louis Chiron, who used one in the Monte Carlo Rally.

Among coach-builders who applied their art to the Type 46 were Van Vooren, Gaston Grummer, Ottin, Weymann, d'Ieteren, Gangloff and, of course, Molsheim. In 1960 an unused Type 46S saloon was discovered in the South of France, stored since purchase. Not surprisingly, Fritz Schlumpf acquired it.

Despite this rash of new touring models, racing had not stopped nor had the racing department experiments. In 1928 they designed the Type 45, principally for hill climbs, but also

Elegant Type 46 fixed-head coupé with sloping windscreen

with a view to formule libre racing. This had a 3.8-litre version of the wartime aero H-16, with two superchargers, roller main bearings and plain big-ends. It was mounted in what was ostensibly a Grand Prix Type 35 chassis, with two-seater pointed tail body. A 3-litre version, the Type 47, was intended for, but never used, in sports car racing. After brief use in 1929-1930 these cars lay neglected at Molsheim until rescued by Fritz Schlumpf. They were restored into pristine condition to be displayed with other 'one-off' Bugatti competition cars.

During 1929 Bugatti was very aware that his cars were being beaten by other manufacturers using twin overhead camshaft engines. His solution was to develop the Types 50 and 51.

The Type 50 was fundamentally the new engine, rather than a complete new car. It had a bore and stroke of 86 x 107mm—4972cc. It retained the fixed-head construction but this now had two overhead camshafts, gear driven, with only two valves per cylinder. It was available with or without a super-charger—an impressive great instrument mounted on the right of the engine. This very powerful engine could be dropped straight into the Type 46 chassis, to become the pure Type 50, or into a lengthened chassis to form the Type 50T. With some 200bhp available at 4000rpm the Type 50 was a fast car, whatever the bodywork.

In various Type 50B connotations this engine was used experimentally in various racing cars run by the works team in formule libre and sports car events. Two are among the line of special racing Bugattis: the 1939 sports car, which used a

development 50B engine in a 1934 Grand Prix Type 59 chassis; and the huge single-seater that Jean Bugatti brought to the Prescott hill climb near Cheltenham in 1939 for Jean-Pierre Wimille to drive. It was the car in which Wimille won the first post-war race in 1945—and the last race to be won by a car entered by Bugatti.

Both the special works cars used a 4.7-litre version of the basic Type 50B engine in supercharged form. Simultaneously, Bugatti was uprating the Type 35 engine to the same formula, retaining the existing bottom end and fitting a new cylinder block and head with two overhead camshafts. In this form, at 2.3 litres supercharged the Type 51 was evolved, with the Type 51A at 1½ litres. There were 2-litre versions, which by analogy have been referred to as Type 51C.

In all other respects the car was the same as the Type 35B. The only obvious outward difference is that the hole in the side of the bonnet for the blower relief valve is lower on the twin-cam cars and the petrol tank in the tail has two fillers. Inside, the magneto, driven from the exhaust camshaft, is offset to the left of the dashboard. The Type 51 was the last word in classic Grand Prix Bugattis, and revived Molsheim's sagging fortunes with numerous fine victories.

Many Type 51s are still in good working order and being used in Historic racing even to this day. Among the sea of blue Grand Prix cars the collection displays two perfect examples of the Type 51 as well as an unusual single-seater version, and a mouthwatering road version with wings, lights and spare wheels.

Top: *Bugatti Type 46 roadster with 5.3-litre eight-cylinder engine*

Above: *Bugatti Type 46S, the Type 46 fitted with a supercharger*

109

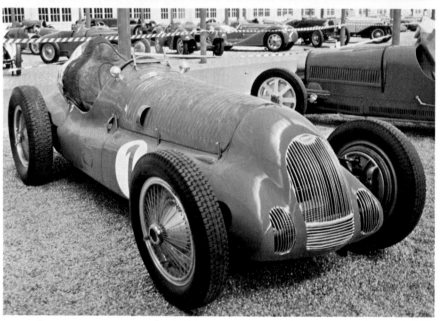

Right: H16 twin-supercharged engine in the Type 47 Bugatti sports chassis. It was related to the early aero engine

Below right: Factory single-seater 4.7-litre Type 50B Bugatti racing car; it appeared once in England in 1939

Below: Type 50B 'Monoplace' winning its last race driven by Wimille

In the same way that Ettore conceived his Grand Sport Type 43 from the Grand Prix Type 35, he evolved the very sporting Type 55 from the Grand Prix Type 51.

The Type 54 was evolved in the line of formule libre activities. It comprised a Type 50 engine of 4.9-litre capacity in a lengthened Type 47 16-cylinder chassis. With 300bhp available in supercharged form, there was more power than the chassis could really deal with.

The basic chassis formed the basis for the Type 55, when a detuned Type 51 Grand Prix engine was installed. With 135bhp it was quite fast and usually carried sporting two-seater bodywork in the idiom of the day—long sweeping mudguards and comfortable cockpit. Only 38 cars were built, mostly with Molsheim bodywork, though the local Gangloff firm at Colmar produced some variations and others built coupés.

The gear-driven twin-cam supercharged engine made a splendid cacophony that was music to the ear of the Bugatti lover. It was very much the sports car of the day and also very 'modern' with two-tone colour schemes of red and black, yellow and black, or white and black.

Top: *Chassis of a Type 53 four-wheel-drive Bugatti racing car; it shows the unusual suspension and drive-mechanism*

Above: *Two Type 53s at the 1932 Klausen hill climb*

Above left: *Type 50 Bugatti with modern bodywork. The engine was the same as for the racing Type 53*

Today a Type 55 Bugatti is a rare treat, so imagine the reaction on seeing seven lined up, glistening in the collection. There are two of the classic open two-seaters, a special bodied open two-seater that has been 'over' bodied, three fixed-head coupés, and a drophead coupé.

Around this time in the Bugatti story there were two diversions, one amusing the other bizarre. These were the Types 52 and 56. Both involved battery power. The first was a half-scale miniature Type 35 Grand Prix Bugatti, built for Ettore's younger son Roland, when he was five, and shown at the Milan exhibition as being suitable for children from six to eight.

It was driven by a normal car starter motor geared directly to the rear axle and energised by a 12 volt battery. It was capable of around 10mph and had proper expanding brakes, cable operated in the best Bugatti tradition, while the wheels carried special Dunlop tyres.

Beside the shrine to Maman Schlumpf are a pair of these miniatures, arranged beside the brothers' full-scale Type 35T, perhaps symbolising a mother and two children.

The second diversion, the Type 56, was for Ettore's own use.

111

Top: *Type 55 Bugatti; the classic model was, like this one, an open two-seater sports car with duotone colour scheme*

Above: *Ettore Bugatti's battery-powered runabout, the Type 56. He used it to travel around the Molsheim factory*

This was a battery-powered runabout in the form of a veteran car with short wheelbase, spindly wire wheels and open body, steered by a tiller. It was designed for getting about the Molsheim factory in comfort and silence. Ettore's personal Type 56 is in the collection among the mid-1930s touring cars. A second was sold in Switzerland, where it is still said to be.

On the racing scene a way-out diversion was the Type 53. This was a huge racing car powered by a 4.9-litre Type 50 engine variant with four-wheel drive. It was intended for speed trials and hill climbs. It was impressive, and accelerated in a straight line, but was a bit uncontrollable when it came to the corners. Two were built without the traditional Bugatti horseshoe radiator shape.

Their use was limited. One appeared briefly in England for a hill climb at Shelsley Walsh, but crashed in practice while Jean Bugatti was demonstrating its remarkable acceleration. From remnants gleaned from the Bugatti factory the Schlumpf brothers have resurrected one of the chassis, which stands bare, without engine or gearbox, revealing all the details of the complex four-wheel drive and suspension.

By the mid-1930s the motoring scene was changing. Car production was, of necessity, more rationalized and Bugatti kept pace with the changes.

The railcar programme was in full swing and the existing range of cars was being gradually phased out; the last to go was the Type 46 in 1936. By 1934 the new era of Bugatti was well under way. The Type 57 series was being designed to provide a one-model range of cars that was to last until war stopped production in 1939.

Jean Bugatti, who in 1934 was 25, was clearly following in his father's footsteps, both artistically and in business. He was influential during the start of what was to prove to be the final phase of the Bugatti empire.

The Type 57 was new almost from front to rear. Basic Bugatti principles were followed, with eight-cylinders, semi-elliptic leaf springs for the front suspension and reversed quarter-elliptics for the rear. Brakes were still cable operated. The twin camshaft

engine had gear-driven camshafts and all bearings were of the plain type. A single dry-plate clutch and a four-speed gearbox in unit with the engine were used. With a bore and stroke of 72 x 100mm this new engine had a capacity of 3257cc and developed around 136bhp in basic form.

Gangloff assisted Molsheim with body production, and closed two and four-door saloons, and fixed and drophead coupés were available. Chassis could be supplied for specialist bodywork.

Production continued from 1934 to 1936 in virtually unchanged form, but a supplementary model was introduced in mid-1935. This was the 57S with a lower and shorter chassis, a dry sump lubrication system, higher compression ratio, special shock absorbers and a V form to the classic horse-shoe radiator. Superchargers were available for increased performance and flexibility, creating the 57C and 57SC—C for 'compressor'.

At the end of 1938 the short-chassis models were withdrawn, and production concentrated on the normal chassis. This was improved with telescopic shock absorbers and hydraulic brakes at long last. They were Bugatti-Lockheed design.

Top: *These sporting fixed-head coupés stand in a row of Type 55 Bugattis*

Above: *Interior of Bugatti Type 57S 'Atalante' coupé*

Body styles remained basically the same, but chassis could still be supplied to specialist coach-builders.

The Schlumpf collection is particularly rich in variations on Type 57. In the 24 versions on display there are normal 57 models, 57C, 57S and 57SC in all their fascinating forms and colours. Many more Type 57s are in the workshops and storerooms awaiting restoration. It was the most popular and rationalized of all Bugatti models.

Among the numerous post-war experimental cars and prototypes retrieved from Molsheim was the car that had been intended to replace the Type 57 in 1940—the Type 64. Jean Bugatti was wholly responsible for it and the car was known as the 'voiture de Monsieur Jean'. The Type 57 engine was enlarged to 4½ litres with the camshafts driven by chains instead of gears. The gearbox was by Cotal and was four-speed, electrically controlled by a tiny switch on the dash. It was the first time any Bugatti had ever used a gearbox not of his own design.

The body was a combination of Jean and Gangloff, with a

Above: *The short-chassis, supercharged 3.3-litre eight-cylinder Type 57SC was the ultimate road-going Bugatti. This 'Atalante' fixed-head coupé is a typical example, one of five 57SCs in the museum*

Far right: *More Type 57 Bugattis; two supercharged 'Galibier' four-door saloons and a Saoutchik-bodied drophead coupé*

Centre: *After the war the Bugatti factory tried to continue production of the basic Type 57, as the Type 101; the combination of the classical radiator shape and modern body did not work*

Right: *Type 57 Bugattis: 'Atalante' coupé; 'Stelvio' drophead coupé; 'Ventoux' four-light saloon*

Above: *1940 prototype Bugatti Type 64 with 4.5-litre eight-cylinder engine and Cotal electric gearbox. It would have replaced the Type 57 if war had not intervened*

Centre: *The 370cc supercharged twin-cam Type 68 was a wartime prototype; an 'austerity' car that finally never happened*

Below: *The Type 252 was the last experimental road car to come from the Molsheim factory, in 1960. A 1½-litre four-cylinder sporting car, it retained the horse-shoe motif in the front grille*

The Bugatti Factory Hoard	
Models from the factory include:	
1911	BB prototype
1912	'Garros' chassis (new) 5-litre
Type 28:	1921 8-cylinder, 3-litre chassis
Type 32:	1923 Grand Prix 'tank'
Type 41:	Royale (Coupé de Ville). Chassis no. 41100
Type 45:	16-cylinder Grand Prix
Type 47:	16-cylinder sports-racing
Type 46:	Coupé
Type 50B:	'Monoplace' racing car
Type 50B:	Sports-racing car
Type 53:	Four-wheel-drive chassis
Type 64:	Prototype. 1940 replacement for the Type 57 series
Type 101:	1950 model
Type 101:	1950 model
Type 251:	Post-war Grand Prix car (two off)
Type 252:	Prototype, 1500cc sports-racing

fashionable 'fast back', and had a V-shape to screen and radiator. It was elegant and would have been ideal if 1940 had proved to be an extension of the 1930s. But it was not to be.

Another rarity on show is the Type 68, designed by Bugatti in 1942 while 'in exile' in Paris. Molsheim had been taken over by occupation forces and was being run by Hans Trippel, a German industrialist who made supplies for the German army.

The Type 68 was intended to be a post-war economy car. It certainly was small, with a 370cc engine, but it had twin camshafts, four valves per cylinder and was supercharged: a little racing engine.

Another project that Bugatti started work on in readiness for the end of the war was a 1½-litre engine, the Type 73, for use in sports and racing cars. All these plans came to nought. Though Ettore retrieved his factory after the war he died in August 1947, at the age of 66. His son Jean had been killed in a road accident just before war broke out, and Roland had not inherited the brilliance of the rest of the family. Roland and the long-serving Pierre Marco tried to keep the car industry going. They produced a handful of pre-war Type 57 cars under the guise of Type 101, but without Ettore the empire was crumbling, and soon to collapse.

The Bugatti name was to appear before the public for the last time in 1956 on an adventurous but misguided Grand Prix car. Lack of money and development doomed it to failure almost from the start. The factory struggled on doing aircraft contract work until its total demise in 1963, when the remaining members of the Bugatti family sent a letter to all the workers. They recorded their grateful thanks for the faith and co-operation shown, and explained that they could go on no longer. They were handing over to Hispano-Suiza.

Mechanical Bugatti display; it features Ettore's initials picked out in superchargers, with an engine and dynamometer in the foreground

RACING

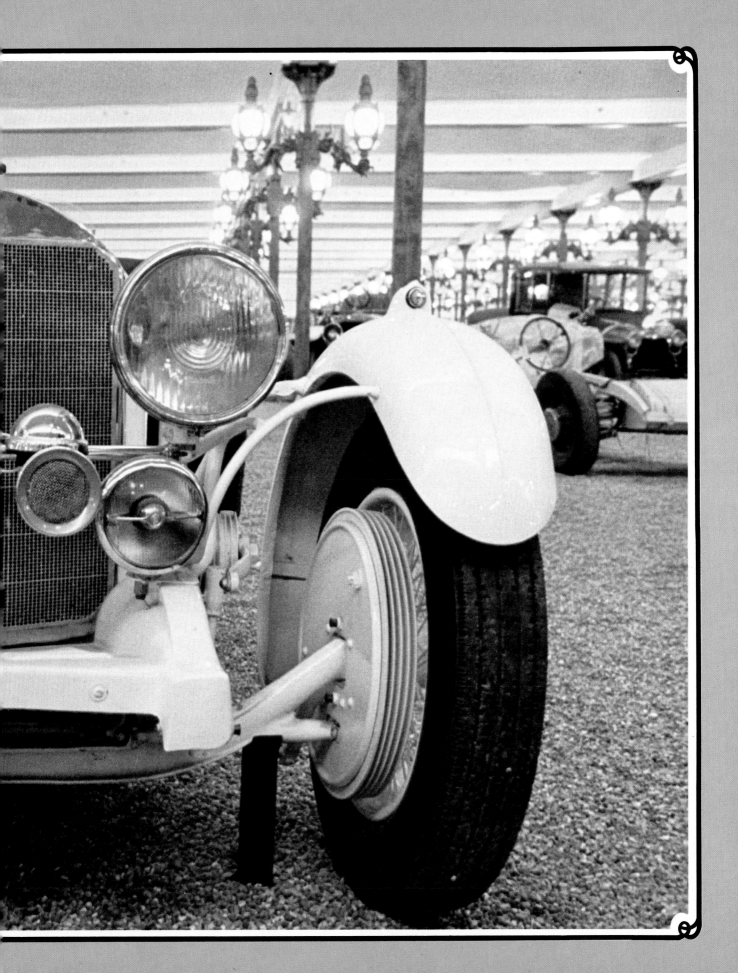

Cars have been raced from the earliest days of motoring. When design was still very much experimental competition offered the perfect arena in which to test new ideas and techniques under the gaze of that select group, the motoring public. It provided manufacturers with the chance to prove their cars were the best.

Early races had little in common with the commercialised and safety-conscious world of modern Grand Prix. Perhaps the biggest difference was that the emphasis was firmly on the cars. Although racing drivers have always been glamorous, even famous characters, it was not until 1950, with the inauguration of the World Drivers Championship, that the spotlight was turned on them. The first races were long distance, high-speed time trials between major European cities: from Paris to Bordeaux, Marseilles or Vienna. However, the danger to people who were not competing soon incurred the hostility of the Press and racing began to switch to closed circuits. These were not the purpose-built race-tracks of today, but ordinary roads from which the public were barred.

There were sometimes classes within the races, but competition cars had not been split into the categories which exist today. Later, as the formulae to which various races were run became more specific, it became impossible for a manufacturer to make one car which could compete successfully in Grand Prix, sports and touring car races. These formulae specified, for example, weight, engine capacity, cylinder bores, single twin or multi-cylinders. Until the 1930s racing for sporting cars was really for touring cars, which took part in such events as the Tourist Trophy and the Le Mans 24 hour Grand Prix d'Endurance. This field apparently held little interest for the Schlumpfs. It is represented in the collection only by Salmsons and Amilcars—French sporting light cars of the 1920s.

After 1930 sports-racing cars began to develop as a separate breed. A gradual relaxation of the Le Mans regulations allowed two-seaters instead of four and they were less strict about cars being catalogued production models. As a result driving a competition car on the road became steadily less feasible. A Type 135 Delahaye, for example, conformed to the regulations of most countries and ran on pump fuel. But the absence of a hood and full windscreen made it impractical for the average man-in-the-street. However, this was a gradual process and the final divorce between 'street' and sports-racing cars did not come until the mid-1950s.

The Schlumpf collection has two cars from the pre-Grand Prix years before 1906—the Serpollet and the Dufaux. The Serpollet is similar to the car which ran in the 1903 Paris-Madrid race. The Dufaux was built for the Gordon Bennett races of 1904.

Leon Serpollet was a pioneer of motor vehicles, even though he believed in steam, rather than petrol. He competed in steam car trials as early as 1888 and by 1890 had travelled from Paris to Lyon, to demonstrate the possibilities of the motor vehicle. He supported all the early motoring competitions, vying with the 'new-fangled' petrol engines and never really bettering them.

In 1902 he recorded the best time in the Nice speed trials at 75.06mph and in 1903 seven Serpollet 'racers' were entered in the Paris-Madrid race. When the accident rate caused the event to be stopped at Bordeaux all seven were still running, though not among the leaders at that point. The origins of the bright blue boot-shaped car in the museum are rather obscure, but it is certainly similar to those that were competing in 1903.

The Swiss brothers Frédéric and Charles Dufaux of Geneva built their first car in the Piccard-Pictet factory and produced the vehicle now in the collection. Typical of the large-engined racing cars of the day, it has eight cylinders cast in two blocks of four, giving a total capacity of 12¾ litres, with final drive by side chains. Called the 70/90 it failed to start in the 1904 Gordon Bennett Cup race after suffering a 'side-slip' on the way to scrutineering. It did manage to set the fastest time in a flying kilometre sprint at Geneva in the same year, driven by Frédéric. A similar car appeared in the French Grand Prix of 1907. It was one of only four straight-eights entered, but retired after seven of the ten laps. The only other known example of this make of racing car is in the National Transport Museum, Lucerne.

The Gordon Bennett races were instigated in 1899 by the expatriate proprietor of the *New York Herald*, James Gordon Bennett, but no one took them very seriously until 1903. They were essentially events between nations. Each country nominated a team of three cars so that in France, for example, there was great rivalry among manufacturers to represent their country. The choice was made by eliminating trials. It was manufacturers' dissatisfaction with the rules that led to the Grand Prix being evolved. The first one, held in 1906, ended the Gordon Bennett races. The instigator took his sponsorship to another form of sport—that of long-distance balloon racing.

The first official Grand Prix was on June 26-27 1906. The rules, written around existing likely competitors, were similar to those used for the Gordon Bennett races. However, they made the competition between makes rather than nationalities, and allowed any number of makes from any one country. This suited the French. A maximum weight of 1000kg was stipulated for this race but this was frequently changed—13 times between 1906 and 1939.

The collection is remarkably representative of Grand Prix cars, with examples of 15 out of the 19 different formulae—the only significant omission is in the 1913-1914 formulae. With the war Grand Prix racing had moved lock, stock and barrel to America and few of the cars returned to Europe. In all the other formulae there is at least one representative and, apart from the 1922-1927 period, the cars are not just Bugattis. With 35 cars from the collection it would be possible to assemble a representative history of the ultimate level of racing design.

The chain-drive Panhard is a 1908 model. Like the Serpollet 'racer' its detailed history is a little obscure. In that year the rules for the Grand Prix, drawn up by the Automobile Club of France, limited the cylinder bore measurements of cars taking part to 155mm for a 'four' and 127mm for a 'six', with a minimum weight limit of 1100kg.

Three of the 12.8-litre, four-cylinder Panhards were entered, but they met with little success. The best placed was driven by

1904 Dufaux built in Geneva for the Gordon Bennett races. Known as the 70/90HP model it has eight cylinders and chain-drive

1909 single-cylinder Delage 'voiturette' racing car

the American, Heath, who finished sixth. Henry Farman retired in another and Cissac, better known as a racing motor cyclist, was killed on the third of eight laps, when his car shed a tyre. This was an important race in Grand Prix history. German cars filled five of the first six places: the only consolation for France was a Clément-Bayard that took fourth. This defeat was so shattering the ACF did not organise another GP until 1912.

'Voiturette' racing took its place, but the cars were not as diminutive as they sound. In 1908 the Grand Prix supporting race had been won by a Delage driven by Guyot at an average speed of nearly 50mph, compared to the 69mph average with which Lautenschlager's Mercedes won the main race. The Delage had a 1178cc single-cylinder engine with dimensions of 100 x 150mm for its cylinder.

By the time the next Grand Prix de l'ACF was staged in 1912, the regulations had been changed. They allowed a free-for-all for

big cars and a simultaneous Coupe de l'Auto for 3-litre 'voiturettes' weighing between 800kg and 900kg. Of the 56 cars entered 42 were contesting the smaller category.

In the larger section Fiat and Lorraine-Dietrich entered developments of their early leviathans with engines double the capacity of the winning 7.6-litre Peugeot. The Fiats were the fastest cars but they were unreliable and victory went to the Peugeot; side-valve Sunbeams won in the 'voiturette' class.

The rules for the 1913 event specified a fuel consumption of 14mpg and a minimum weight limit for the big cars of 800kg. Peugeot were again successful, finishing first and second with 5.6-litre cars, ahead of a 4½-litre side-valve Sunbeam. For the 3-litre category, the Peugeot designer Ernest Henry produced a variation on the twin-cam design. This smaller unit influenced the later engines of Bugatti and Sunbeam.

Ernest Henry and Peugeot had made a remarkable and

Rare 1921 Ballot racing car with 3-litre straight-eight cylinder engine with twin overhead camshafts

successful transition from the leviathan racing car to the small sophisticated model in a very short time. The racing world naturally took a close look at the winning 1912 and 1913 twin-cam Peugeot engines and many designers copied them. Only one example is known to exist in Europe, a 1913 model in a collection in Bordeaux.

Collectors of historic cars, and especially historic racing cars, would give anything to acquire a 'Henry' Peugeot. The Schlumpf collection has the next best thing: a 3-litre straight-eight Ballot, of 1920

After the war Ernest Henry left Peugeot and joined the Ballot factory in Paris. He designed racing cars for the Indianapolis 500-mile race of 1919, and then 3-litre cars, ready for the revival of Grand Prix racing in 1920. In fact, racing in Europe had to wait another year.

The rich blue Schlumpf Ballot looks a little out of place among a miscellaneous collection of Amilcars and Salmsons and a BNC sports. It would be difficult to know where else to place it. It is

such a rare piece that it would stand out no matter what its neighbours were.

For 1914, the Grand Prix formula was set at 4½ litres and a maximum weight of 1100kg. The race attracted nearly 40 entries from all over Europe. Mercedes, Sunbeam, Vauxhall and Delage were among those who attempted to break the Peugeot domination established by the firm's top driver Georges Boillot. The Grand Prix was held on a hilly circuit at Lyon which placed a premium on braking efficiency. Four-wheel brakes made their appearance on Delage, Peugeot, Fiat and Piccard-Pictet. This last Grand Prix before the First World War saw the Mercedes team sweep the board—but not before Boillot had put up a terrific fight with a Peugeot.

During the war years the Grand Prix machinery went to America. Here the battles of 1913 and 1914 were continued between Mercedes, Peugeot, Sunbeam and Delage. Peugeot were more often victorious.

The Americans naturally learnt from the invasion. The

Mid-1920s Mercedes Benz SSK sports

European cars were ahead of those of the United States. An ironic side-effect of the competition between them was a successful foray into European racing by the American Duesenberg team at the French Grand Prix of 1921: Jimmy Murphy took on and beat the might of the works Ballot team at Le Mans, driving the whole race unaided, although he had broken some ribs in a practice accident. He fought the car over the last lap and a half, with water gushing from a hole in the radiator and its tyres shredded by the appalling road surface. The French showed their normal bad grace in defeat. As in 1914 at Lyon, they refused to play the winner's national anthem and Murphy was awarded a modest medal for his heroic drive. The Ballot driver received a huge second-place trophy. The American invasion was a one-off affair. Not until 1967 would another American win a Grand Prix in an American car.

With the motor car and its manufacture spreading throughout Europe it was not surprising that other countries wanted major national races. The Grand Prix which had started out as a French affair, gradually became an international occasion, with Belgium, Italy, Spain, Germany and many more countries joining in. The Italians started the ball rolling with their Grand Prix in 1922, the Spaniards spread the word in 1924.

The period between the wars was one of enormous progress in racing technology. Improvements in metallurgy and the increasingly sophisticated use of supercharging boosted power outputs to levels unimaginable in 1922. Similar advances were made in streamlining bodyshells. The introduction of features such as independent suspension and hydraulic brakes also had a dramatic effect on car performance.

It was not only the quality of the engineering that improved. As the motor car became a part of more peoples' lives, the scale of Grand Prix racing increased. As the Second World War approached the sport, like everything else, fell under the shadow of Nazism. Hitler realized that it provided the perfect fodder for his propaganda machine—"*Deutschland uber alles*". No expense was spared to ensure total dominance by the Mercedes-Benz and Auto Union teams in the years before 1939.

For 1922 the French, who dictated the Grand Prix formula, decided to reduce the capacity limit to 2 litres, as if to ward off a possible American 3-litre foray. It was successful. The Americans decided not to join in for the first year and kept to the 3-litre formula for their own races. The 2-litre formula lasted from 1922 until the end of 1925. It is represented in the collection by various Bugattis, and the 1924 Targa Florio type Mercedes which competed in just one 2-litre Grand Prix, the 1924 San Sebastian race. After the First World War, the Germans were so unpopular in France and Belgium that their cars were banned for several years—when Mercedes decided to concentrate on sports cars.

The Type 30 was the first straight-eight production Bugatti and, although not considered one of 'Le Patron's' best, it provided a good basis for a 2-litre formula Grand Prix car.

It had been planned to hold the first post-war Grand Prix in 1921 at Strasbourg, but this was postponed for a year because of local opposition and was run at Le Mans instead. When it finally took place at Strasbourg in 1922 the entry was very good. There were three cars each from Fiat, Sunbeam, Ballot and Rolland Pilain, four from Bugatti and two from Aston Martin.

Ernest Henry's influence was everywhere. The Ballots were developed touring cars he had designed before he moved to Sunbeam, where he was responsible for their Strasbourg entries. The Aston Martin 'four' was reputed to have been a direct copy of Henry's Peugeot engine, sold to them by his successor, Gremillon. The Fiats were six-cylinder versions of the straight-eights which had been run the previous year; the Sunbeams were classic Henry long-stroke fours; and the Rolland-Pilains were unimpressive.

Then there were the Bugattis. The Type 30 had a novel cigar-shaped body and an exhaust system that pushed the gases out through the end of the pointed tail. It was no match for the Fiats. Only two-thirds of the entry reached the finish with Felice Nazzaro's Fiat 57 minutes and 52 seconds ahead of de Vizcaya's Bugatti, at an average speed of 79.2mph. The victory was so conclusive that only Bugatti turned up for the Italian Grand Prix.

Meanwhile in Sicily, a vast team of Mercedes had arrived to contest the Targa Florio non-formula race, one of the few races open to them. They brought a pair of developed pre-war cars, a pair of production 'sixes' with superchargers and a pair of 1½-litre supercharged 'fours'. The supercharged cars did not win, but it was a foretaste of what was to come. For 1923 Mercedes decided to build a team of supercharged 2-litre cars for the Grand Prix races they were allowed to enter.

*One of the earliest Bugattis the
Schlumpfs' workshops restored was this
very rare Type 45 Grand Prix
16-cylinder*

Amilcar Six with supercharged 1100cc twin-cam engine; a delightful example of a French 'voiturette' racing car

By 1923 Indianapolis had accepted the 2-litre limit and two European teams—Bugatti and Mercedes—entered. Bugatti had single-seater bodywork on Type 30s, which was not allowed under the European rules. Mercedes had full two-seater bodies on their supercharged 2-litre cars. Today it seems scarcely credible that broadly similar cars could take part in races over both the purpose-built raceway at Indianapolis, and the twisting, badly surfaced roads of the Targa Florio. It shows just how specialised modern racing has become.

The Bugattis suffered from con-rod breakages. Even so, de Vizcaya was running fifth at 450 miles when his car stopped. Mercedes fared slightly better. One car ran third for a while, but their final placings were eighth and tenth, sandwiching the best Bugatti in ninth. Victory went to an HCS-Miller, and Miller-engined cars took the first four places.

After Indianapolis George Duller demonstrated the effectiveness of the Bugattis' streamlining. He achieved new records at one mile and five miles, with speeds of 105.55mph and 104.89mph. To put this remarkable performance into perspective, a modern 2-litre Ford Cortina could just about match it.

Bugatti continued his streamlining efforts on the model for the 1923 French Grand Prix held at Tours: the Type 32, known as the 'tank' because of its odd appearance; its outline was similar to armoured military tanks used at the end of the war. The Schlumpfs acquired one of these cars from the Bugatti factory. The earliest known Grand Prix Bugatti extant, it heads the line of 15 subsequent Grand Prix Bugattis on the stand near the

1924 Mercedes supercharged 2-litre four-cylinder 'Targa Florio' model, in chassis form

museum's entrance. Its strange crablike appearance contrasts jarringly with the imposing row of classic Bugattis with their horse-shoe radiators and pointed tails. The Type 32 was unsuccessful, more because of its mechanical details than its shape: but its attempt to 'cheat the wind' made it a landmark in racing car design. Strangely, Bugatti did not return to the streamlined shape until 1936, when he built 'tank'-bodied sports cars for long-distance races such as Le Mans.

The Type 32 had completely slab sides, a fastback and a matching 'fast front'. The only differences between the front and back were that the front had a slot for a radiator air intake and the starting handle protruded, while the back had a protruding exhaust pipe. The steel bodywork was rather crudely made with flat surfaces and sharp edges.

The cars were amazingly short, with a wheelbase of 6½ feet, shorter than that of a modern Mini. Their narrow (3ft 4in) track caused problems for the drivers and mechanics as they did not sit on the road very well. The occupants sat with their legs alongside the unguarded eight-cylinder engine which protruded back into the cockpit. Unlike the Type 30 these cars had quarter-elliptic leaf springs at the front as well as the rear, and carried the gearbox in unit with the rear axle. Although four entered for the Grand Prix only the one in the Schlumpf collection has survived complete. The remains of another were retrieved from Czechoslovakia by an English collector.

The car had a reputation for poor handling but it is not known whether this was due to its shortness, as is usually suggested, or

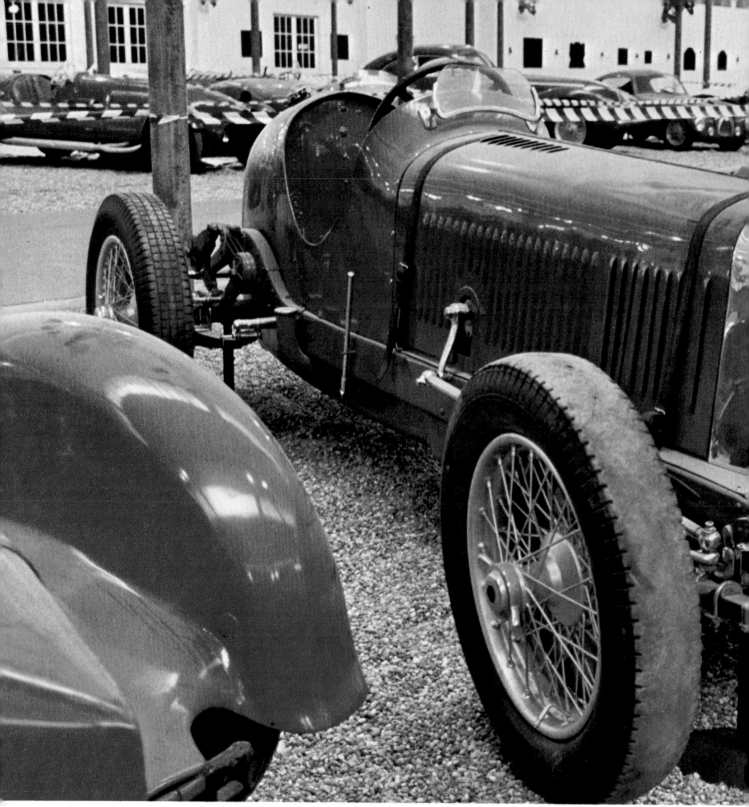

The 'Phi-Phi' Etancelin 1934 Maserati 8CM, chassis number 3010; it has a supercharged eight-cylinder twin-cam engine

the relatively massive bulk of the rear axle hopping from crag to crag on the bumpy roads of the time. Gabriel Voisin entered four wedge-shaped, aerodynamic cars in the racing car class after the authorities had turned them down as touring cars. Their sleeve-valve engines did not have enough power to give their drivers a chance of taking the lead. There was a single entry from Delage with a formidably complex V-12 engine. The French were also represented by three cars from Rolland-Pilain, one of which used an unusual 'cuff-valve' engine by Ernest Schmid.

The Sunbeams and Fiats led the opposition to the French. The Sunbeams were designed by the ex-Fiat designer Bertarione and were referred to as 'the Fiats in green paint'. European racing was still a patriotic affair with all the teams painted in their national colour: dark green for England, blue for France, white and then silver for Germany, and red for Italy.

The Fiats were clearly fastest in the race around 35 laps of the

14.2 mile circuit outside Tours, but they had problems with their superchargers. The unfiltered air intake was too close to the track and picked up stones which wrecked the engines.

In the end it was left to Henry Segrave's cannily driven Sunbeam to come through to win from Albert Divo in another Sunbeam, and Ernest Friderich in the first of the Bugattis.

There was constant rivalry between manufacturers to catch and keep the outstanding designers and engineers. In 1923 Fiat who had lost Bertarione to Sunbeam, also lost Carlo Bazzi to Alfa Romeo. There he joined Merosi in the newly-formed racing department under Enzo Ferrari. Alfa Romeo also lured Vittorio Jano from Fiat; he produced the supercharged Types P1 and P2 Alfa Romeos. All the manufacturers were hard at work perfecting the superchargers which dominated the 1924 racing. The Fiats, with Roots-type superchargers instead of the vane-type Wittig, used their increased power to win the Italian Grand Prix at

Monza in 1923, after the P1 Alfa Romeos were withdrawn because of a practice accident.

Mercedes won the Targa Florio with developed versions of their 1923 Indianapolis cars. They defeated the supercharged Fiat 502SS 1½-litre cars and some modified road-going Alfa Romeos. The Targa chassis in the Schlumpf collection could well be an Indianapolis car, or it could be one of the 1924 team.

The chassis was fairly conventional with semi-elliptic leaf springs all round. The gearbox had four forward speeds and the rear axle still featured the double crown-wheel and pinion layout of the 1914 cars. The supercharger was vertically mounted on the nose of the crankshaft and blew its air through the carburettor. This was necessary because Mercedes did not want the supercharger to be in permanent use.

The 1923 Cremona race marked the first appearance of the P2 Alfa Romeo. This used an engine similar to that of the 1923 Fiats. It was said to produce 165bhp at 5500rpm, with 10psi boost from its supercharger. The cars were certainly fast and were timed at over 123mph. Inevitably they won, and established themselves as contenders for the French Grand Prix.

At the 1924 San Sebastian Grand Prix Segrave won in a Sunbeam despite stopping to help at the scene of an accident to his team-mate Kennelm Lee Guiness. As a result of this accident, riding mechanics were banned from Grand Prix racing in 1925. Bugattis took fastest lap and finished second, fifth and sixth, with Delage third and fourth.

Five of the new Bugatti Type 35s were entered for the French Grand Prix of 1924 at Lyon. Their rivals were the Sunbeams, now supercharged, the P2 Alfa Romeos, the Fiats and the unblown Delage V-12s. All of these had considerably more than the 100bhp which the unsupercharged Bugattis could muster.

The Sunbeams suffered magneto troubles in the race, the Fiats had brake problems, the Delages went well and an Alfa Romeo won. The Bugattis never had a chance; their new wheels and tyres were a constant problem with thrown treads and cracked wheels. The race was won by Campari's P2 Alfa Romeo after Ascari's failed to restart following a last-lap pit stop. Delage took second and third, with another Alfa fourth and Sunbeam fifth.

The Type 35 described in the Bugatti chapter was the start of an entirely new line of thinking by Ettore, especially as regards chassis and bodywork. The basic layout of the straight-eight cylinder engine was not changed. It received much publicity at Lyon, but as a debut for a new car it was a disaster.

In 1925 Fiat were largely absent from the scene and the Delage was finally supercharged to match the P2 Alfa Romeo at 190bhp. Bugatti, still refusing to use the supercharger, had to accept that the only way his cars could win was through reliability. They were not placed in the major European events, but Costantini won the Targa Florio and Masetti the unimportant Rome Grand Prix.

The organising body for Grand Prix at this time was the Association Internationale des Automobile-Clubs Reconnus (AIACR) which was reconstructed in 1947 as the present-day Fédération Internationale de l'Automobile (FIA).

For 1926 it decided that the 130mph achieved by the fastest cars was too high on the road surfaces, and the capacity limit was reduced to 1.5 litres. A side-effect was to put Bugatti in an impregnable position. Alfa Romeo were disenchanted, and Delage and Talbot were building complex new machinery.

Bugatti, meanwhile, had built a few Type 35s with 1.5-litre engines, by reducing the dimension of the cylinder bore from 60mm to 52mm. These were easily supercharged for the formula. Later the Type 39 was to replace these modified 35s and use the much superior dimensions of 60 x 66mm. Bugatti won the European Championship with little opposition. In doing so, he won nine Grand Prix.

Meanwhile, the Delage designer, Albert Lory, had produced a radically fast straight-eight. It was unable to show its promise in its first season, but in 1927 the bugs had been eliminated and it was victorious wherever it appeared. The chassis was never brilliant, but the engine design was so advanced it was still winning races ten years later.

Delage provided only a temporary challenge to Bugatti. The onset of the Depression caused virtually all the works teams to withdraw, leaving only privately owned Delages, Alfas and Maseratis to challenge the French cars. The steady divorce between touring and racing cars during the 1920s meant that separate design programmes were needed for each. This was simply too expensive for manufacturers in dire financial straits.

Maserati was a new name on the scene. Alfieri Maserati had been an engineer at the Diatto works. Diatto had made Bugatti aero-engines during the war, built the 16-valve cars under licence immediately after 1918, and then produced their own versions. The Diatto straight-eight engine was the basis of the first Maserati in 1926, as the 1.5-litre Tipo 26.

With so few manufacturers able to afford to take part, the 1½-litre formula rules were dropped in 1928. Events ran to a free-for-all law, or formule libre as far as capacity was concerned. There were a few detailed limitations on weight, but even these were dropped in 1930. Formule libre continued until 1934. During this period Bugatti provided most of the competitors, both the factory team and the private owners. The main opposition came from Alfa Romeo and Maserati. The earliest Maserati in the Schlumpf collection is a 1931 Tipo 8C-2500. At this time racing cars were still built as two-seaters though riding mechanics had long since been barred.

Of the nine major races in 1928 Bugatti won six. By now the most frequent winners were the Types 35B (supercharged 2.3-litre) or 35C (supercharged 2-litre). The B and C versions were ultimately developed into the Type 51, with twin-cam engine, to keep the cars competitive against the Italian opposition. During this formule libre period Bugatti experimented on the side with cars made for the popular and less extravagant activity of mountain hill climbing, rather than for serious road racing. The remarkable H-16 Type 45 was built in 1928. Its engine had two banks of eight cylinders standing side-by-side on the crankcase. Each bank had its own supercharger.

The Type 47 was a sports version of this car. It was intended

for Le Mans, but was never completed. Two of the racing cars took part in some hill climbs, but were soon abandoned. They lay derelict in the Bugatti factory until Fritz Schlumpf acquired them and resurrected one Grand Prix car complete, and the sports car complete less its bodywork.

These two remarkable collector's items, in pristine condition, stand proudly at the head of a display that contains numerous factory racing cars from the Molsheim works. Alongside this unique line is the chassis and drive mechanism of another car that was a product of the formule libre period, when Grand Prix was at its lowest ebb.

The French were greatly interested in mountain hill climbing and Ettore Bugatti supported them with his works drivers. He built the Type 53 in 1932, with its 4.7-litre engine and four-wheel drive. Two of these cars were constructed.

Most attention was naturally focused on full-scale Grand Prix

racing, but 'voiturette' racing was still in full swing as a second-class form of racing. The supercharged six-cylinder Amilcar in the collection personifies these 1100cc events. It was developed from a long line of four-cylinder 'voiturettes', of which a pair of CGSS sports models are on display. Their great rivals, the French Salmsons, Senechals and BNC are also shown.

To get even with the twin overhead camshaft Salmson, Amilcar designer, Edmund Moyet, and his assistant, Pierre Chan, evolved the little 'sixes'. They were helped by a Sunbeam engineer who provided drawings of their 2-litre cars.

The design followed twin overhead camshaft practice with the cams driven by a train of spur gears at the rear of the engine. Dry sump lubrication involved two oil pumps. The supercharger was driven from the nose of the crankshaft; two types were tried according to whether the 56 x 74mm or 55 x 77mm configuration was used. Twin rotors were one above the other for the

Opposite top: *Maserati 8C Grand Prix car in action in 1934*

Opposite lower: *1931 Maserati 8C-2500 in sports form—a Grand Prix two-seater with wings and lights*

Below: *1937 Mercedes-Benz*

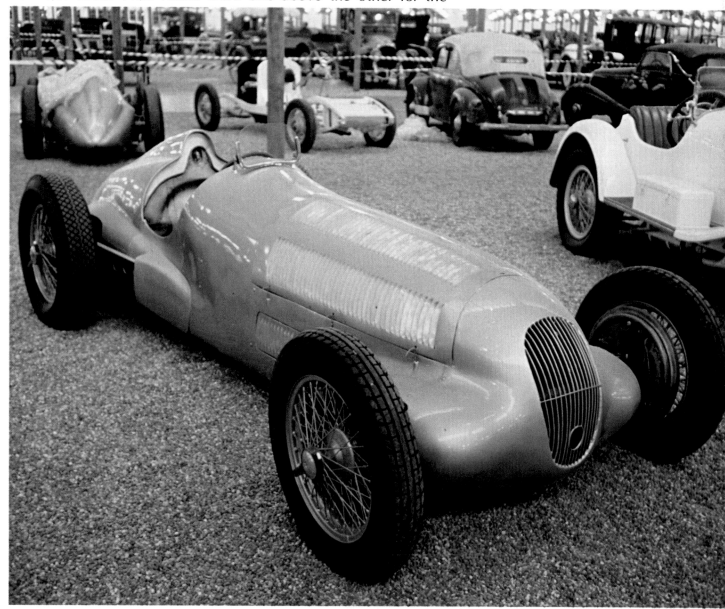

latter, and side by side for the former. Power output from the 1100cc unit with the 56mm bore was 107.5bhp at 6750rpm.

A deep frame was built up for the chassis with its cross-members bolted in reamed holes. Semi-elliptic springs were used on the front suspension, the rear had trailing quarter-elliptics and a torque tube. These watch-like little cars were so successful that a road-going version, the C6, was also built. Its output was 62bhp at 5600rpm with a smaller supercharger and other engine modifications.

From 1931 to 1933 the Bugattis were challenged by the 'Monza' Alfas (2.3 and 2.6-litre straight-eights) and, a later development, the famous 'monoposto'. Maserati first introduced their challenger, the 8C-2500, in 1930. This was one of the more successful 1930 cars. Before the appearance of the Type 51 Bugatti it gained seven victories in 1931 against the ageing Type 35 Bugattis and the 1750cc sports Alfas.

The Maserati followed Italian practice, with supercharged straight-eight engine developing 175bhp at 6000rpm. The chassis used semi-elliptic springing all round and a torque-tube in the final drive. A great deal of 'Elektron', cast by the

1939 Mercedes-Benz V-12 cylinder W163 Grand Prix car without body panels; behind it is a complete sister car

Isotta-Fraschini company of Italy was used in the engine and braking system.

Rules for 1931 had merely stipulated that no mechanics were to be carried and that Grand Prix events should last ten hours. For 1932 this was reduced to between five and ten hours, and for 1933 to a race distance of 500km.

Maserati produced a new model for 1933 of 3-litre capacity, called the 8C-3000, C for 'Corsa' or 'racing'. The engine was similar to that of the 2500 with a narrower crankcase and a higher compression ratio to give 210bhp at 5600rpm. The first two 3-litre cars were two-seaters although the rules did not require this. The rest were 'monopostos' and were designated 8CM—eight-cylinder 'Corsa Monoposto' or 'racing single-seater'. The chassis was so narrow, with only 20 inches between the side rails, that the frame tended to whip and make the cars skitter alarmingly down the road. This was altered to a wider chassis for 1934 and this became the Maserati contender.

Alongside the 1931 8C-2500 in the Maserati display at Mulhouse stands a venerable 8CM. This is number 3010 which was sold to the French driver from Rouen, Philippe Etancelin

141

Above left: 1936 Alfa Romeo V-12
cylinder Grand Prix car; it was changed
into a two-seater for sports car events
and raced in Switzerland until
1953-1954

Above: Alfa Romeo 2900B in Mille
Miglia coupé form, with Pininfarina
styled front

Left: Bugatti factory special
sports-racing car of 1939; it was built
around a modified Type 59 Grand Prix
chassis and running gear with 4.7-litre
Type 50B engine

('Phi-Phi' to his friends), who raced it extensively throughout 1934 and 1935. He drove in shirt sleeves with a peaked cap worn back to front, as he had done in the past when racing various Bugattis. When Etancelin joined the Maserati works team the 8CM was put away in his country home, where it stayed until he gave it to a small museum nearby during the 1950s. It passed into the Schlumpf collection comparatively recently and now keeps company with a row of racing Maseratis.

Etancelin had a most successful season with the car during 1934 before joining the works team. He won the race at Dieppe, finished second at Nice, Casablanca and Montreux, third at Vichy and fourth at Tripoli. The car has certainly earned honourable retirement among the many other famous cars at Mulhouse.

The 1934 formula was to see great changes in the Grand Prix world. Mercedes-Benz and Auto Union, used and encouraged by Hitler as a symbol of national superiority, were to prove far superior to the opposition, mainly Bugatti and Alfa Romeo.

The new rules had been decided as far back as the winter of 1932. They imposed a 750kg maximum weight limit and a minimum body width of 34 inches leaving the designers a completely free hand with engine capacity. The formula was intended to last for three seasons.

Bugatti continued with the Type 59, introduced in 1933, but the engine capacity increased from 2.8 to 3.3 litres. Alfa Romeo used a developed version of the Tipo B with a 2.9-litre engine developing 255bhp at 5400rpm. The other contender to line up for the first event at Monaco was the Maserati 8CM. Guy Moll won in the Alfa Romeo. But the German opposition hotted up. In 1932 Hitler had offered DM40,000 (about £20,000) to any firm who developed a national racing car. With this sort of subsidy both Auto Union and Mercedes-Benz set to with a will.

Mercedes-Benz were generally on top, except for 1936 when they had technical problems and let Auto Union in for a whole season. The real trouble with the rear-engined Auto Union was that only two drivers, Berndt Rosemeyer and Tazio Nuvolari, ever mastered it—and Nuvolari preferred to drive Italian when there was something Italian worth driving.

Auto Union followed the 'tear-drop' Benz design of 1923 with a mid-mounted V-16 engine of 4.4 litres developing 290bhp at a gentle 4500rpm. The car featured independent suspension all round with trailing links at the front and swing axles at the rear, carried on a tubular frame and encased in a body made from aluminium and doped fabric.

The Mercedes-Benz equivalent was the W25 with a front mounted 3.4-litre supercharged straight-eight developing 354bhp at the beginning of the season, but rising to 430bhp when the capacity was increased to 4 litres. The suspension on a boxed-channel frame used wishbones at the front and a swing axle at the rear.

First of the major confrontations was the German Grand Prix at the Nürburgring. Mercedes-Benz won, followed by Auto Union and Chiron's Alfa Romeo. Alfa took the Penya Rhin Grand Prix with no opposition before the teams moved to Montlhéry for the

French Grand Prix. Bugattis, on their home ground, were eclipsed by the German cars and the Alfa Romeos. The Tipo B proved to have the speed to take on Mercedes and Auto Union. It eventually took first, second and third place after the Germans had wilted.

This was only a temporary setback for the silver cars. The Belgian Grand Prix went to Bugatti whose cars had the legs of the Alfas in an encouraging reversal of fortunes. The Germans did not compete. At Pescara Mercedes-Benz were victorious when Guy Moll, who was leading the field in the Tipo B, crashed and killed himself. At Berne it was the turn of Auto Union; Dreyfus held second for much of the race in his Bugatti but lost a place to another Auto Union when he stopped for water. Alfa Romeos took fourth and fifth.

At Monza, Mercedes-Benz dominated and were trailed home by Alfa Romeo. No Bugatti was entered. At San Sebastian Mercedes-Benz were again first and second with Bugatti hard on their heels. The final race of the season saw an Auto Union win, followed by Mercedes-Benz and Maserati.

By now it was almost all over for the non-German teams. Only Nuvolari in the Tipo B Alfa was able to threaten the German might. 'The Flying Mantuan' used all his skill to stay with, and even beat, Mercedes-Benz and Auto Union. He drove in his usual dramatic style sitting well back from the wheel and "almost dancing from side to side in the cockpit."

For 1936 Alfa Romeo had produced a 4-litre V-12 for their Tipo 8C with the alternative of a 3.8-litre straight-eight. The V-12 developed 370bhp, the other 330bhp. Auto Union had increased the capacity of their V-16 to 6 litres and 520bhp, while Mercedes-Benz had a shortened W25 with 4.7 litres and 494bhp. It was the year when Mercedes-Benz had nothing but problems; the dominance of Auto Union was threatened only by Nuvolari's Alfa Romeo.

Mercedes-Benz had prepared the W125 for the new 3-litre formula which should have arrived in 1937, but which was eventually postponed for a year. They also brought out a bigger, stronger 5.7-litre straight-eight which developed a colossal 646bhp on the special racing fuels allowed at the time. In mid-season they developed superchargers which inhaled through the carburettors rather than blowing through them. They improved the suspension, retaining the wishbone system at the front, with a de Dion axle at the rear running behind the gearbox differential unit.

Auto Union retained a similar design to 1936, but managed to keep up with the more powerful Mercedes-Benz through the sheer virtuosity of their young driver, Berndt Rosemeyer. Like Nuvolari he had started as a motor cycle racer, but had a unique ability to handle the unwieldy Auto Unions. He gave his employers four of their five wins in major races that year. Another five went to Mercedes-Benz and a solitary victory went to Pintacuda's V-12 Alfa in Rio de Janeiro.

The new Alfa was the Tipo 12C with 4½ litres and 430bhp in a lower shape. It still was not really competitive.

Of the cars of the 750kg formula, the Schlumpf collection

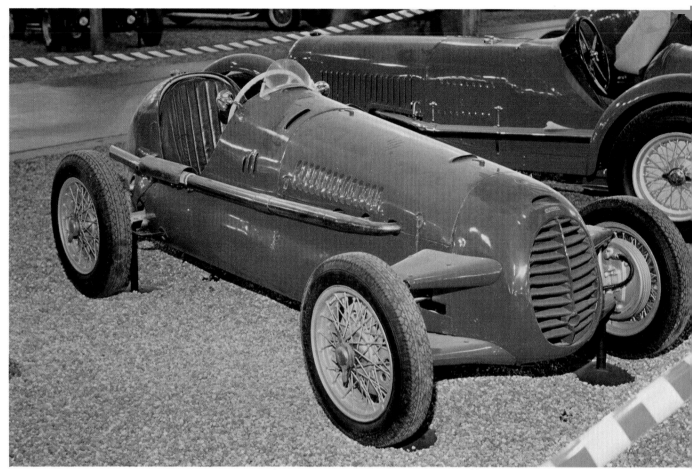

1946 Cisitalia D-46 single-seater; it was built around Fiat components to provide a cheap and simple form of racing

contains two rare specimens as well as the 8CM Maserati. These are a 1937 Mercedes-Benz and a 1937 Alfa Romeo V-12, two of the giants of the golden age of brute force. It would only need an Auto Union to complete the scene, but only one is known to have survived and that is in Germany. Neither the Mercedes-Benz nor the Alfa Romeo are in original condition. They were modified in 1938 when the Grand Prix formula was changed, for use in other forms of competition.

The W125 Mercedes-Benz, one of the cars modified for mountain hill climbs such as the Grossglockner and the Schauinsland, came from the Stuttgart factory in an exchange deal. The Alfa Romeo was converted into a two-seater sports-racing car in Italy and was acquired by the Swiss amateur driver, Willy-Peter Daetwyler after the war. It was successful in national races and hill climbs from 1949 to 1954 and was rebodied by the Italian coach-builder Michelotti in 1953. It stands in this form alongside two other sports Alfa Romeos.

The new formula for 1938 allowed unsupercharged cars to have 1½ times the engine capacity of those with superchargers, giving 4½ instead of 3 litres. This option was taken up by Talbot with a 'six' and Delahaye with a V-12; both produced about 200bhp, about half the power of the German cars. Bugatti returned with a 3-litre version of the Type 50B engine in a modified Type 59 chassis carrying a suitably streamlined body. Alfa Romeo were to be seen with new cars, the 308 and 312, with a 295bhp straight-eight and a 350bhp V-12.

The German onslaught was based on the W154 Mercedes-Benz and used a similar chassis to that of the previous year, with

a 60 degree V-12. Auto Union also chose 12 cylinders, but with a 90 degree V-12 which required three camshafts instead of the one used in the V-16. The mid-engined cars followed Mercedes-Benz in adopting a de Dion rear axle.

In the opening Grand Prix, at Pau, the Delahaye confounded the opposition by winning—no Auto Unions and only one Mercedes-Benz were entered—and followed up with a win at Cork. The Bugatti was there, but no German cars. After that it was Mercedes-Benz and Auto Union all the way with the balance in favour of Mercedes-Benz after Rosemeyer died at the start of the season in a record-breaking attempt. It was only when Nuvolari was persuaded to leave the Alfa team that Auto Union again had a driver capable of taking on the talented Mercedes-Benz team—Caracciola, von Brauchitsch, Lang and Dick Seaman. Nuvolari gave Auto Union two wins.

Mercedes-Benz produced another new model for 1939, the W163. This was an aerodynamic improvement on the W154 and also had another 60bhp by using twin superchargers in series rather than in parallel. In this final season of German domination, Mercedes-Benz were the more successful despite Nuvolari's virtuosity. Sadly Dick Seaman, the wealthy British driver who ranks as one of the all-time greats, died from burns sustained in a crash in the Belgian Grand Prix. Britain had lost her foremost driver. It was fitting that Nuvolari won the final Grand Prix before the Second World War, at Belgrade. He stood out through the 1930s as being the greatest driver. Born in Mantua in 1892 he was over 40 when he drove that final race for Auto Union.

Top: *The Gordini Le Mans coupé driven by Fangio and Gonzales in 1950*

Above: *Gordini coupé supercharged 1½-litre at Le Mans in 1950*

147

Bugatti built two Type 73C single-seaters in 1947 but neither progressed beyond the chassis stage. This one is still incomplete; the second, in the English Donington Park collection, has been finished with a 1939-style body. Significant features are the supercharger on the nose of the crankshaft, the huge inlet pipe, and the starting handle on the side of the chassis

The Schlumpfs' tribute to the abbreviated 3-litre period, which the war stopped, is two of the W163 Mercedes-Benz. They were acquired through the brothers' personal friendship with Alfred Neubauer; the doyen of team managers, he was still in charge of the next Mercedes-Benz Grand Prix effort, in 1954.

The formula that was to follow the war had its roots in pre-war 'voiturette' racing with a 1½-litre limit. The British had not produced a Grand Prix car since the Sunbeam of the 1920s, but were well to the fore in the 1930s in the smaller class, with the ERA—English Racing Automobiles.

Maserati were producing the highly effective, supercharged four-cylinder 4C. The first appeared as early as 1930 with a 65 x 88mm twin-cam engine in the original straight-eight chassis. A lightweight single-seater followed as the 4CM-1100, then for 1932 came the 69 x 100mm, 1496 4C-1500, which developed 130bhp at 5500rpm.

Maserati and ERA were often protagonists in 1935. ERA had the less dated engine and in response Maserati introduced the 6CM in 1936. This had a new 65 x 75mm engine supercharged to produce 155bhp—about the same as an early ERA.

The new Alfa Romeo Tipo 158s appeared for the first time in 1938. These were called 'Alfettas' and used a supercharged straight-eight engine and all-independent suspension. The engine was basically half the V-16, which had been tried in the 308 chassis, and produced 195bhp at 7000rpm—too much for the ERAs and Maseratis. Maserati again produced a new engine.

They, too, used half their Grand Prix engine for the new model, the 16-valve 78 x 78mm 4CL, which produced a claimed 220bhp. Its chassis retained the torsion bar front suspension but used splayed trailing quarter-elliptic springing for the rear axle.

By 1939 these cars were already as fast as the 4½-litre unsupercharged cars of Grand Prix racing, but they were all put into the shade by the new Mercedes W165, produced in a very short time for the 1939 Tripoli Grand Prix. Part of the reason for the 'voiturette' formula's success had been its freedom from German domination, so this new contender was anything but welcome—particularly when it made the other cars look obsolete. It featured a 64 x 58cc V-8, supercharged to produce 260bhp and later, with twin blowers, 278bhp, and ran away with the Tripoli race. This prompted Alfa Romeo to increase the boost pressure on their supercharger to get 225bhp. But such measures were superfluous. War was declared.

After the war, the new Grand Prix formula logically equated these one-time 'voiturettes', with the 4½-litre unsupercharged cars. In the years that followed Grand Prix racing changed almost beyond recognition. Within ten years nearly all the great names of the inter-war period— Bugatti, Alfa Romeo and Mercedes-Benz—had retired from Grand Prix racing. They were replaced first by Ferrari, Vanwall and BRM, and later by a whole new breed of manufacturers such as Lotus and Cooper.

But the post-war period started with one of the 'old firm' dominating—Alfa Romeo. Apart from 1949 they remained top

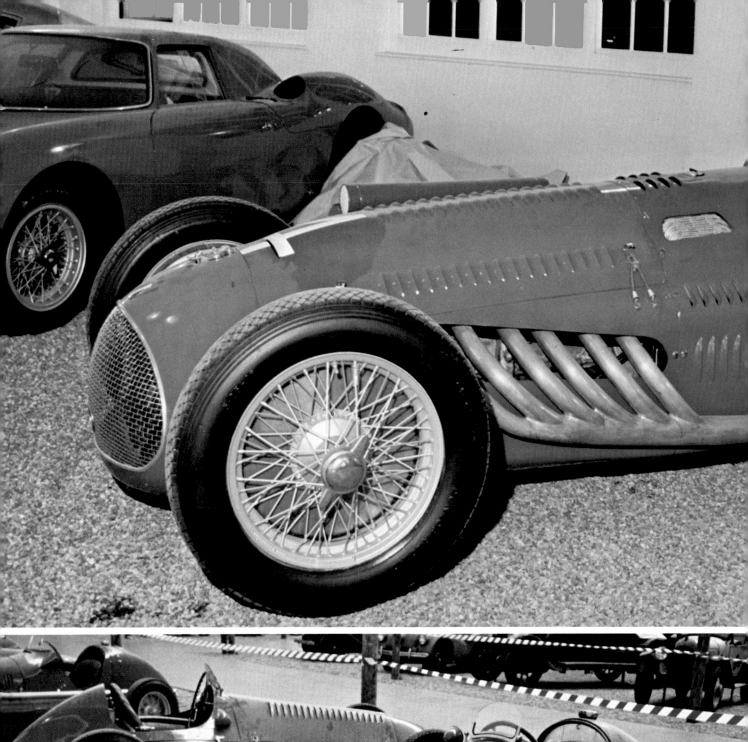

until the middle of 1951, when their twin-stage supercharged engines were producing around 400bhp—enough to push the cars along at 180mph. Maserati developed their 4CL with twin-stage supercharging from 1947. However they were never a match for the Alfas, although they dominated the races where only a host of pre-war ERAs turned up. With the 4CLT/48 came the tubular chassis and a much lower, sleeker shape.

Meanwhile, one of the great racing *marques* was being born. Enzo Ferrari, who was team manager for Alfa Romeo and had evolved the design of the 158 with Gioacchino Colombo, had started producing his own cars, with Colombo. This was the start of the V-12 lineage which became synonymous with Ferrari. Alfa Romeo were away for 1949 and Ferrari's supercharged V-12 1½-litre cars were running well.

The big 4½-litre straight-six Lago-Talbots were an even match, while the 4CLT/48 Maseratis made the early-season running with three victories. Two were for the man who was to go on to win more world championships than any other, Juan Manuel Fangio. Lago-Talbots took two victories and the Ferraris the remaining five.

Alfa Romeo returned for 1950 with the 158s but Ferrari responded by introducing an unsupercharged 3.3-litre V-12 giving around 300bhp. By the end of the season the engine had grown to a full 4½ litres, giving 350 bhp.

All was not well in the Maserati camp. Their twin-stage supercharged 'fours' had been no match for Ferrari the previous season, and the introduction of the 4CLT/50 with a little more power did not help Scuderia Argentina, which was

Above: *Philippe Etancelin at Silverstone in 1950 in a 4½-litre Lago-Talbot*

Above left: *4½-litre Lago-Talbot Type 26 Grand Prix car of 1949-1951; these unsupercharged cars upheld French honour against Ferrari and Maserati just after the war*

Left: *The Maserati 4CLT/48-50 driven by Dr Guiseppe Farina when he was not racing for the factory Alfa Romeo team*

campaigning these cars. A further development was made by a private Milan team, Scuderia Milano. They used a large single Roots-type supercharger and eight-plug heads to produce 330bhp in a 4CLT-type chassis.

The story of 1950 and early 1951 was Alfa Romeo's attempts to stay ahead of the Ferraris. Driven by the 'three Fs', Fangio, Farina and Fagioli, they won all the races they entered in 1950, with six to Fangio and four to Farina. The Tipo 159 was introduced, with more power and a de Dion rear axle to keep Ferrari's 'Prancing Horse' at bay.

In the 1951 British Grand Prix at Silverstone the unbroken run of 27 Alfa Romeo victories was ended by José Froilan Gonzales, 'the Pampas Bull', in a Ferrari. The spell was broken at last, and Ferrari and Alfa Romeo shared the remaining four races of 1951.

The Schlumpfs' selection of cars from that six-year period includes a Maserati 4CL from 1947 and a 4CLT/50, a pair of the big 4½-litre Lago-Talbots from 1950 and the car that changed the pattern, a Ferrari 4½-litre V-12.

The museum does not have a Tipo 158 Alfa Romeo, but neither does any other outside Italy. The Milan factory has all their cars.

Alfa Romeo withdrew at the end of 1951 and it was generally accepted that the only way to get competitive fields for the Grand Prix races was to run them for Formula 2 cars, the equivalent of the pre-war 'voiturettes'. This formula for unsupercharged 2-litre cars had been running concurrently with Formula One, with a wide variety of teams. Ferrari had been using a 2-

1955 Mercedes-Benz 300SLR sports-racing car on permanent loan to the Schlumpf museum; this model dominated racing during its short one-season life

litre V-12 and there were a number of British cars—particularly Cooper-Bristol and HWM.

Maserati produced their six-cylinder A6GCM for 1952. This stemmed from the work done on the post-war A6. Ferrari started with the V-12 but decided to revert to a four-cylinder. The only car to uphold the racing honour of France was the Gordini, but no one could challenge Ferrari, whose Tipo 500 was all-powerful for the two seasons of the 2-litre formula.

Just one car from that period would tell the tale and the Schlumpf collection includes a Ferrari 500. But it also includes a massive selection of Gordinis.

Amédée Gordini was born in Bologna in 1899. He settled in France in 1926, setting up a business to tune and maintain the Fiats being built by Simca. In the early 1930s he started rallying and then turned to motor racing.

Le Mans was the main outing for any Frenchman, and, in 1937, when Bugatti won with the 57G, there were five Simca entries—three Simca-Fiats and two Simca Cinqs of 996cc and 596cc respectively. Three of them retired but a Cinq came 17th overall and sixth in the Index of Performance. This was an efficiency formula that took into account the size and output of the car in relation to its average speed in the race. Gordini did exceptionally well in the 1938 and 1939 Le Mans, winning the Index both times.

These performances in the Index were an indication of Gordini's ability, which Simca recognised after the war with a firm contract. Among the many Gordini cars in the collection are

Above: *The Type 251, designed by Colombo, represents the Bugatti factory's last attempt to enter Grand Prix racing, in 1956. Its transverse mid-engined layout was very advanced. A sister car, without body panels, stands alongside revealing technical details*

Far left: *This Maserati 250F Grand Prix car started life with a V-12 cylinder engine which was subsequently replaced by a six-cylinder*

Left: *Amédée Gordini's early 1937 sports-racing car*

One of the last Gordini Grand Prix cars; minus its one-piece body it shows details of the 2½-litre eight-cylinder engine

the 1939 Index winner, a Simca 8, and the Gordini car driven by Gordini himself in 1937. One of his earliest cars, it is known as 'La Grandmère'.

After the war Gordini set up his own company, Equipe Gordini, with considerable backing from Simca, who wanted him to promote their name in racing. The first car produced used the Simca-Fiat 1100cc overhead valve engine in a strong little chassis with wishbone front suspension and a torsion bar sprung live rear axle. It weighed only 318kg and with 65bhp was good for 110mph. Jean-Pierre Wimille recorded some good performances in the car against such rivals as the D46 Cisitalia, one of which is also in the collection.

An enlarged version with 1430cc and a cross-over push rod valve gear system was good enough to give Gordini a couple of Formula 2 victories in 1948-1949 with Fangio and Trintignant at Marseilles and Perpignan. Simca then backed the building of a twin overhead camshaft supercharged 'four' with 78 x 78mm 1496cc dimensions. This gave Trintignant a victory in the non-championship race at Albi.

Four Simca-Gordinis were entered for Le Mans in 1950: two open cars with the unsupercharged 1½-litre and two coupés with supercharged engines. The one that did best was a coupé driven by Fangio and Gonzales, which ran in ninth place for three hours. This coupé is in the collection.

All four 1½-litre entries in the 1951 Le Mans failed. Simca withdrew support and the cars became simply Gordinis. Gordini then designed a stretched version of the 1½-litre for the new formula in 1952, using 75 x 75mm dimensions for a 2-litre six-cylinder. This was mounted in a new torsion bar sprung chassis, and the team made a three-pronged attack with Behra, Trintignant and Manzon. They achieved placings but no victories in their first year; the cars suffered from axle failures.

The following year was little better, although Trintignant achieved two victories in non-championship races in France. One of these Formula 2 cars is in the collection.

The new Formula One for 1954 was for unsupercharged cars up to 2½ litres. Gordini stretched his 2-litre 'six' to 2½ litres, as did Maserati with their 250F developed from their old Formula 2 car. The new Maserati marked a change in chassis design. It had a tubular space frame and a de Dion rear end in place of the old quarter-elliptically sprung live rear axle. One of the early 250Fs, entered by Scuderia Centro-Sud, is in the collection.

Gordini kept to his live axle for 1954. Like everyone else, he was trounced by the all-conquering straight-eight Mercedes Benz W196. One of his 1954 cars is on show.

Midway through the following season Gordini produced a new car. This was an all-independently sprung, disc-braked chassis carrying a straight-eight engine of 75 x 70mm bore and stroke. With four twin-choke carburettors it was claimed to produce 250bhp, although it probably gave rather less.

Other teams were also over-optimistic in their power figures. They all tried to keep pace with the quoted 270bhp of Mercedes-Benz.

Gordini's new car was not a success. The old 'sixes' were

often used as standbyes over the next couple of years. At the end of 1957 Renault offered Gordini the job of modifying their saloons and he retired from Grand Prix racing. His two 1957 eight-cylinder cars are in the collection, one without bodywork.

The Schlumpfs have a number of his sports-racing cars. When Gordini retired from racing he gave various cars to French museums but the bulk was presented to the Schlumpf collection. Restoring the cars to Schlumpf standard, at their expense, was the last task undertaken by head mechanic, Robert Aumaitre and the Equipe Gordini.

The collection also includes a representative selection of the sports cars against which the Gordinis competed. Inevitably, there are Ferraris from the days of V-12s and 'fours' developed from the Formula One of the time.

There is also a Maserati 300S, developed from the Formula One 250F, and a Mercedes-Benz 300SLR—one of the all-conquering sports cars that competed alongside the equally successful W196 single-seater Grand Prix car from the Stuttgart firm. This car is one of the few out of Daimler-Benz captivity. It was part of a deal that involved the W163 cars, and some veteran Mercedes.

The Alfa Romeo 'Disco Volante', or 'flying saucer', is a sports car unrelated to a Grand Prix car. The Milan factory produced it when they stopped racing the 159s. Five were built in 1952, three 2-litre four-cylinders, and two 3-litre six cylinders, all with twin overhead camshafts.

They were never raced by the works in 'flying saucer' form, but the 'sixes' were run in 1953 with only a victory to Fangio in the Supercortemaggiore Grand Prix at Merano, against the works Lancias. The car in the collection is one of the original 2-litre models, which was used by the Swiss driver Jean Ducrey for local events around 1954-1955.

Two more cars in the collection from the 1954-60 Formula One are the ill-fated Colombos-designed Bugatti Type 251 cars. One ran in the French Grand Prix of 1957, driven by Maurice Trintignant. It was much slower in practice than the opposition—Ferraris, Maseratis and Vanwalls—and a seized throttle control put it out after 18 laps. In fact this was a promising debut, but there was no money to develop the car further. In that its transversely mounted straight-eight engine was mounted amidships, it heralded the forthcoming mid-engined revolution. A revolution typified by the little Cooper-Climax cars that won the championship in 1959 and 1960, and the Lotus 18, one of which is in the collection.

The two Type 251 Bugattis are displayed side-by-side, one complete with bulbous blue bodywork, the other stripped of all the panelling so that the transverse engine, the unusual non-independent suspension, with telescopic shock absorbers, and the tubular space frame can be seen.

The 1½-litre formula introduced in 1961 was designed to slow down the cars once again, but by 1965 the suspension development saw to it that these little cars were faster round circuits than their larger predecessors.

Three cars in the collection typify that period, which started

Far left: *The V-6 cylinder Ferrari (above) and Lotus 25/33 with V-8 Coventry Climax engine (below) depict the 1961-1965 era of 1½-litre Grand Prix racing*

The 1952 Alfa Romeo 2-litre 'Disco Volante' (above) and the V-8 engined Spanish Pegaso (left) also of 1952 were short-lived sports cars

Ferrari 250LM coupé with 3-litre V-12 engine mounted behind the driver; this successful layout, developed from the Le Mans Ferraris, is now universal in sports-racing cars

with Ferrari domination. They were the only team ready. The Ferrari shown is not one of those early 65 degree V-6s, but a later 1963 120 degree V-6.

Lotus are also represented with two of the Climax V-8 cars of the type in which Jim Clark demonstrated his great skills. The Lotus 24 was used by the Swiss, Jo Siffert, and represented the last of the space-frame cars used in 1962. This was the customer version of the car that Lotus built for themselves—the revolutionary, monocoque Lotus 25. This construction which did away with all the old tubes and their relative flexibility, was eventually adopted by every major racing constructor.

Alongside the Lotus 24 is a final development of the Lotus 25 monocoque car in the form of a Lotus 33. This ended the 1½-litre formula years for the English firm, which was undoubtedly one of the 'trend-setters' of the 1½-litre era.

The first World Drivers Championship had been won in 1950 by Dr Guiseppe Farina in an Alfa Romeo. Over the years, the battle between the drivers rather than the cars has become the main focus of Grand Prix racing.

With the exception of the evergreen Juan Manuel Fangio, racing drivers started to reach the top at a younger age. Farina was 44 when he won the championship, while Ascari was looked on as a relative youngster when he became champion at 34. The trend downwards started with dashing Mike Hawthorn and continued in the mercurial careers of Moss, Clark and Stewart, all of whom reached the foreground of Grand Prix racing before their 30th birthdays.

The whole character of Grand Prix racing has been transformed. With the exception of Ferrari few of the teams can any longer be said to represent any particular national interest. As a result racing has become a self-contained travelling circus with 15 or 16 races a year in locations as diverse as Japan, South Africa and Canada—supported with vast injections of money from firms that have no direct connection with the industry.

As the drivers assumed a central importance, their safety

became the major concern, and the classic circuits of the past are rarely used.

Technically, and visually, there have been many changes. Rear-engined cars have become universal as have disc brakes and fully independent suspension. Much of the progress has been in aerodynamics and tyres.

The final modern Formula One car in the collection is the Ferrari 312B, first of the flat-12 Ferrari Grand Prix cars in which Ickx almost wrested the 1970 World Championship following Jochen Rindt's death during practice for the Italian Grand Prix.

On the sports car front, the Schlumpf story winds up with a Ferrari 250LM. It was developed from the 250P sports car that won at Le Mans in 1963. The other sports car is a Porsche 907—a regular Le Mans runner in this form with its long tapering tail with a small wing at the end. These cars were first used in the 1968 season with the 2.24-litre flat-eight engine.

Two cars at Mulhouse support the view that racing improves the breed: a Mercedes-Benz 300SL from 1955 and a 1960 Ferrari 250GT, both of which had competition successes but were essentially road-going cars. The 300SL stemmed from the Le Mans winner in 1952, part of Mercedes-Benz early foray after the war. The Ferrari was the Italian firm's contender in GT racing and had many successes in this form.

The Pegaso, also in the collection, was built in the old Hispano-Suiza works in Barcelona between 1951 and 1958. Only about 125 were made. The first showing was at the Paris Salon in 1951 with a 2½ litre, four overhead camshaft V-8 and a five-speed rear mounted gearbox in conjunction with a de Dion tube. The engine size was gradually stretched up to 3.2 litres, before being replaced by a push rod 4 litre V-8, itself enlarged to 4.7 litres. The cars only competed in local Spanish events and the firm returned to making commercial vehicles in 1958 when their designer, Wilfredo Ricart, retired.

It is questionable whether the Schlumpf brothers deliberately set out to represent Grand Prix history. But close study of their museum provides a rare opportunity to inspect 64 years of racing development.

Racing produced some memorable personalities and brilliant engineers whose names are still recalled through their cars. The road cars of today undoubtedly owe many of the features that are taken for granted to the risks and inventions forced on designers by the need to keep ahead of their rivals. So the collection gives a valuable perspective on the modern car. More than anything it shows how car design has changed over the years. It is almost impossible to believe that the sleek red Ferrari 312B has anything in common with the leviathans of the early Grand Prix days—but the scope of the Schlumpf collection makes this contrast possible.

THE BEST OF THE REST

Sadly, it is not possible to feature every car in the Schlumpf collection in the various specialised chapters of this book. Here are the best of the rest.

Far Left: *Protos, 1912*

Above: *Mercedes-Benz SSK, 1928*

Left: *Alfa Romeo 'Zagato' supercharged 1750cc*

Below: *Amilcar Type CGSS (far left); Gordini 2½-litre eight-cylinder Grand Prix car, 1957 (centre); Mercedes-Benz 300SL 'Gull Wing' coupé, 1955*

Top: *Bugatti Type 43 with special bodywork*

Right: *BNC 1100cc, about 1926*

Below: *Mercedes Type 28/95*

Top: *Alfa Romeo 2900B with abbreviated Swiss-built bodywork*

Left: *Bugatti Type 51 with road equipment*

Below: *Alfa Romeo drophead coupé 1750cc, about 1930-1931*

GRAND TOURING

The most outstanding exhibits in the Schlumpf museum are two Bugatti Royales. These cars represent the culmination of Ettore Bugatti's efforts to achieve an ultimate 'Grand Tourer'; a car that has no equal in luxury, style and precision engineering.

The Italians invented the words *'gran turismo'*, to distinguish high performance cars with closed coach-work from the more spartan 'sports car'. The French, however, used the term 'voiture de Grande voyage' or 'Grande Routier', meaning a car for touring in the Grand Manner. The long, straight Routes Nationales encouraged this form of motoring, in what is called a 'long-legged fashion'. Italy and Germany were beginning to evolve special motor roads, the Autostrada and Autobahn and touring in the Grand Manner was becoming part of the scene in those countries as well as in France.

In Britain there were no such roads, or distances, and any touring was inevitably in 'the small manner'. This could be why there are few Grand Manner cars from the British industry in the museum. The only examples are Rolls-Royce and Bentley. A remarkable selection from the European market is displayed. Mercedes-Benz, Horch and Maybach from Germany; Farman, Voisin, Hispano-Suiza and Bugatti from France; Isotta-Fraschini and Lancia from Italy.

The period between the wars saw the brief flowering and virtual demise of the true Grand Touring car. Before the First World War travelling fast by road had imposed spartan standards of comfort. Today's so-called Grand Tourers have neither the space nor the smoothness of their predecessors.

Motoring in the Grand Manner was only possible in an age of individualism. At that time many car builders made only the chassis and mechanical components. The bodywork was left to specialists. Many of these coach-builders had learned their skills in the days of the horse-drawn coach, and the lavishness and luxury of the 'gentleman's carriage' was often reflected in the steel and aluminium of the 'bespoke' bodywork of a Rolls-Royce, Hispano-Suiza or Bugatti Royale.

Some manufacturers had their own bodywork departments, but even then customers had a choice of body styles and could select individual details such as upholstery, lamps, additional instruments or equipment. As a result, the designers and engineers could express their creativity in their cars. There were none of the constraints imposed by a mass market.

The aim was to produce cars that were the epitome of grace, style and speed. A wealthy owner expected to be able to whisk his family in perfect comfort from Paris to Cannes, with no chance of seeing an identical car on the way, or, worse still, of seeing a similar one on arrival.

Bugattis in the Grand Manner dominate the Schlumpf collection. The Types 41, 46 and 50 are all stylish models, saloon or coupé, with plenty of room inside; yet they are fully capable of top speeds as high as 100mph—real Grand Touring performance. Their rakish lines successfully prove the point that the Bugatti style was as well suited to the Grand Manner as it was to pure racing.

For sheer extravagance there is nothing to compare with the

magnificent Bugatti Royale (or Type 41). Only six were built, between 1927 and 1933; the first remained the personal property of Ettore Bugatti. It was rebodied many times, starting life as an open tourer and finishing with exotic Coupé de Ville bodywork, probably inspired by Ettore's son Jean.

This Royale, chassis number 41100, remained in the Bugatti family until long after Ettore's death. It was finally acquired by the Schlumpfs when the Molsheim factory closed and the brothers bought Bugatti's own collection. In addition to this unique Royale, the Schlumpf collection also has number 41131, a vast sombre saloon, as dull and ordinary to look at as 41100 is exotic and elegant.

Its body was built by the English firm of Park Ward to the special requirements of Captain C.W. Foster in 1933. The interior was the last word in comfort and English style. Captain Foster kept the car for 13 years; each year he sent a Christmas message to Ettore Bugatti: "All is still well with the car."

After the war the 41131 passed into the hands of Jack Lemon-Burton, a London Bugatti fancier; it was often seen at Bugatti Owners Club meetings during the 1950s. Eventually it was sold to the American collector John Shakespeare, and in 1962, it passed into the Schlumpf collection together with 30 other Bugattis.

With a wheelbase of over 14 feet, a seven-foot long bonnet and a crankshaft weighing all of 356kg, the Royale was the leviathan of its age. The engine needed to propel this huge machine at its maximum speed of a claimed 125mph was of classic Bugatti construction. It consisted of a 12.8-litre straight-eight with three valves per cylinder—each cylinder with the same capacity as a modern Ford Cortina. With a single overhead camshaft it produced 300bhp at a leisurely 2000rpm.

The car was a commercial flop. At a cost, with bodywork, of around £6500, at a time when an average house cost £500, it is hardly surprising that there were few buyers—especially when maintenance was such a problem. Even replacing a valve, normally a straightforward operation, meant that the whole Royale engine had to be removed and stripped.

The idea of the Royale was conceived before the First World War and its engine design was probably based to some extent on the Bugatti H-16 aero engine. In this it was similar to Hispano-Suiza, Voisin, Farman and Maybach practice. Their designers all had connections with the aeroplane industry.

Gabriel Voisin, for example, turned to car design at the end of the First World War when he took over an 18cv Citroen design which the company had decided to abandon in favour of small mass-produced family machines. The first Voisin was powered by a four-cylinder Knight sleeve-valve engine and stayed in production until 1926.

Voisin's cars became increasingly more sophisticated until in 1929 he introduced 4-litre and 5-litre V-12 engines; he still used sleeve valves in a car with distinct aircraft tendencies about its body design, of which the collection has one example.

Because Voisin made the bodywork for his cars—he viewed them as a single design unit—he never really competed with the

Above: *The Bugatti Royale limousine, with body by Park Ward of London, built for Captain C. W. Foster in 1933 on chassis number 41131; only the elephant mascot on its radiator cap, and the clock from the centre of the steering wheel, are missing*

Far left: *Ettore Bugatti's Royale, often called the 'Coupé de Patron' but in fact a Sedanca de Ville. One of the most elegant of the Royales, chassis number 41100 had four body styles before this*

Left: *Interior of Ettore's Royale*

1932 Voisin saloon with V-12 engine; Voisin always built his cars with his aeronautical background in his mind

great chassis builders and their friends the coach-builders. Nonetheless, he tried hard to conceive cars for touring in the Grand Manner.

The English-born Farman brothers were active in competitions at the turn of the century. Like Voisin, they were involved in the early aircraft world. After the First World War, they too tried car production, and began with the A6 family leading finally to the NF models.

All were well constructed, using six-cylinder engines of 6.6 and eventually 7.1 litres. The chassis formed an ideal base for the coach-builders. The two examples on display are A6Bs from about 1924. One is a large limousine and the other a Coupé de Ville, or Coupé Chauffeur.

Near these Farmans is a pair of magnificent Hispano-Suizas—one of the great *marques* in the Grand Manner epitomising the ostentatious, but tasteful, tradition of that style of motoring. Marc Birkigt, the Hispano-Suiza designer, also used

his wartime aero engine experience in the design of the H6 model, which appeared in 1919.

The Farman brothers tried to provide motoring in the Grand Manner with this six-cylinder 1924 model

The alloy-block, overhead camshaft engine produced 135bhp from its 6.6 litres giving a maximum speed of over 80mph. Although the engine looked attractive, it was less quiet than many of its contemporaries. The basic crankcase casting extended sideways out to the chassis side-members to make a polished aluminium floor for the engine compartment. Above it the cylinder block and cam box were in stove-enamel black. Many of the ancillary services were totally enclosed to complete the picture of clean simplicity.

Although the H6 continued into the 1930s Marc Birkigt was keen to produce a more sophisticated car. The result was a smooth 9½-litre V-12 which produced 220bhp at 3000rpm in its original form. It was unusual in its 'square' cylinder dimensions, with identical bore and stroke measurements of 100mm. In the search for more power and torque, to propel heavier and more

Top: *Hispano-Suiza provided cars with a sporting character for owner-drivers who wanted to indulge in Grand Touring; the later V-12 engined cars such as this one gave smooth, effortless travel. A V-12 engine stands alongside*

Above: *A pair of Grand Tourers: Isotta-Fraschini from Italy (left) and Farman from France*

luxurious bodywork, this already massive engine was enlarged to nearly 11½ litres in 1934 when the power increased to 250bhp.

These magnificent V-12 machines are displayed 'as a pair'; between them is a gleaming V-12 Hispano-Suiza engine. The two cars are a yellow-and-black saloon and a red-and-white Vanvooren Coupé. When an example of the Vanvooren Coupé was tested by the English press in 1934, it achieved nearly 100mph, and accelerated from standstill to 60mph in 12 seconds. Even with a light body, such as the drophead coupé, it turned the scales at nearly two tons (2032kg) and needed powerful brakes to stop from such speeds. Birkigt's servo-assisted system, developed on the H6 model, still proved up to the job.

One of the German rivals to the Hispano-Suiza was the Maybach. The W3, a 5.8-litre six-cylinder with side valves

Above: *1935 Maybach Zeppelin V-12 cars were noted for their solid appearance*

Left: *1938 Maybach Zepplin V-12 with Cabriolet body style; a rare car*

developing 70bhp at 2200rpm, set the German firm on the Grand Manner path. This car incorporated some of Wilhelm Maybach's unusual ideas on the ultimate in easy driving. He believed that the hands should stay firmly on the wheel, so foot pedals controlled not just the accelerator, brake and clutch, but also the choice of high or low gears and reverse.

In the far corner of the Mulhouse museum, almost overshadowed by more exotic or exciting makes, is a unique collection of Maybach models, mostly from the early and mid-1930s. Among them are two examples of the ultimate Maybach, the Zeppelin. One is from around 1934 and has limousine bodywork; the other from around 1938-1939 has the popular German style of Cabriolet bodywork. For this *tour de force* Maybach built a V-12 cylinder engine, that grew to 8 litres

The Mercedes-Benz 7.7-litre Grosser model was the ultimate in engineering from the Stuttgart firm. This 1938 Cabriolet model is very rare; many of these cars carried saloon bodywork with bullet-proof glass

in the final models. It was claimed to produce 200bhp—sufficient to push the three-ton car along at 100mph.

Another unusual feature of the Maybach was the way the transmission became progressively more complex. In 1921 two gears had been thought enough for the 5.8-litre W3. By 1938 the V-12 had a fantastically complicated system that gave eight forward speeds and, if required, four reverse. This was contrary to the thinking behind every other design, where it was assumed that more power meant fewer gears were needed.

Whatever their idiosyncrasies, the Maybachs were beautifully made and offered supremely comfortable, if ponderous, transport. In Germany the leading members of the Nazi party seemed to prefer Mercedes-Benz. The Maybach Zeppelin was a car for bankers, industrialists and aristocrats. Herbert von Dirksen, the last German ambassador to the Court of St James before the Second World War used one. As with Hispano-Suiza, the chassis makers depended on the coach-builders for the final look of their cars. They were seldom let down.

The obvious rival to the Maybach Zeppelin was the Grosser Mercedes-Benz, or model 770. This car had a straight-eight, 7.7-litre engine rated at 150-200 horsepower depending on

The 1938 Mercedes-Benz Grosser chassis was impressive with its supercharged eight-cylinder engine, all-independent suspension by coil springs, and tubular chassis

whether the supercharger was engaged or not. It was the standard vehicle of senior members of the Nazi party and favoured by Hitler himself. Other customers were heads of state, including Emperor Hirohito of Japan, one of whose two examples was still in use until recently. Orders for these cars, which were nearly always built in armoured versions, totalled only 117.

The car remained in the same form from 1930 to 1938, when it was completely redesigned. The new model was longer and carried wishbone front suspension with swing axles at the rear, like many Mercedes-Benz since. Production was even more limited and only 82 were made.

In an imposing array of Mercedes-Benz of the 1930s, including 500K and 540K roadsters, the Schlumpfs climax this era of German design in the Grand Manner with a rare Cabriolet version of the 7.7-litre Grosser of 1939. Behind it, as if to explain the Grosser mechanical concept, is a complete chassis with no bodywork. These two exhibits illustrate just why these cars were a pinnacle in designing for the Grand Manner.

The main difference between the Mercedes-Benz and cars like the Hispano-Suiza is that the German cars were designed for

Above: *A rare V-12 Horch Type 600; it has an elegant drophead coupé body and unusual three-piece windscreen*

Far left: *Mercedes-Benz roadster; it was a cross between a sports car and a Grand Tourer with the looks of the former and the character of the latter*

Left: *Mercedes-Benz 540K; it was the final word in opulence. Bodywork is by Erdmann & Rossi of Berlin*

179

muscular chauffeurs to wrestle with, rather than for owner-drivers. They often weighed as much as 3½ tons (3570kg), had no power steering, and drove like trucks. Most enthusiasts would far rather have the 500K or 540K models in the collection, which were usually more attractively styled, and more fun to drive.

The 500K was introduced in 1934 with a 5-litre engine producing 100-160bhp, dependent on the use of the super-charger; it was just capable of 100mph. In 1936 the 540K was introduced. The early straight-eight engine was given more power and the top speed increased to 105mph. These cars were attractively, and more luxuriously styled but were never as fast as they looked, and certainly never rivalled the older SSK series.

A basic two-seater roadster style of body was offered on the 540K, though there were specialist variations, including Cab-riolet models. The handsome white roadster in the collection, which epitomises this era of motoring, has a body by Erdmann & Rossi of Berlin.

Another German contender in the Grand Manner stakes was the Horch. The firm was founded by August Horch in 1900, after he had worked for Karl Benz. Later following a disagreement with fellow directors over his tendency to build high-performance cars, August Horch started the Audi firm.

The Horch company had already established a reputation for making sound sports-tourers when Paul Daimler, son of the famous Gottlieb, joined the staff in 1923. Daimler's first design was the Horch 300, a 2120cc straight-eight with two overhead camshafts and long-stroke dimensions. Over the years the engine was enlarged to just under 4 litres in the 375 model, giving 80bhp at 3000rpm.

None of the 300 range was particularly appealing. They tended to overheat and the long-stroke layout was rather dated. A new engine was designed by a group of engineers including Fritz Fiedler and Rudolf Schleicher—both to become part of BMW. The new design was the 450, a 4½-litre straight-eight with only one overhead camshaft. A change of stroke gave alternative engine sizes of 4 or 5 litres.

As the 450 - 850 series was developed its suspension became much more sophisticated. It had started with conventional semi-elliptic leaf springs all round but changed to independent front suspension with twin transverse lower leaf springs and an upper link; a jointed axle with leaf springs was sometimes used at the rear. The 853 model looked similar to the 500K Mercedes-Benz, but wasn't as fast. It weighed 2 tons (2032kg) and, with only 105bhp, was pushed to exceed 85mph.

Between 1931 and 1933 Horch produced a new model, the 600-670 series. This had a new V-12 engine, and used a similar chassis to the earlier cars, but without the independent suspension. Although this V-12 was much smoother than the 'eights', it was no more powerful, and did not make the motoring any grander, apart from its smoothness and silence. Production was relatively small, so it is the more interesting to see a drophead coupé version in the Schlumpf museum. This imposing red-and-black coupé has the distinctive three-piece windscreen, with curved ends, to give a wider range of vision.

In 1932 Horch joined the Auto Union combine, along with Audi, Wanderer and DKW. At first this did not make any noticeable difference to their products. The symbol of these four makes became the four linked rings which are displayed on Audi cars to this day. This merger or combine, was a Depression-inspired salvage operation conducted by a Dane, Rasmussen.

Neither Audi nor Wanderer ever made the Grand Manner market, though they did combine to attempt this with a front-wheel-drive model produced by Audi, using a six-cylinder Wanderer engine. It was built in the Horch factory, to Horch standards and general appearance. Like the Horch it looked good but was overweight for its power output.

Alongside the magnificent V-12 Horch drophead coupé, stands a pale green-and-black Audi drophead coupé. It illustrates nicely how the Audi-Wanderer combine failed to match the 'elder statesman' image. While it would have looked imposing enough on its own, it looks insignificant alongside the Horch. Perhaps the Schlumpfs positioned it deliberately.

Apart from looks and grandeur, the poor Wanderer engine of 2411cc produced only 55bhp, so that the car could barely reach 70mph. The suspension was rather inefficient and the front-wheel-drive caused heavy steering. Altogether this car was barely a pale imitation of Grand Manner models produced by other manufacturers.

In the far corner of the museum stand three majestic Isotta-Fraschinis, a large saloon and two Coupé de Ville Tipo 8A models, leviathans of a great Italian age. In Italy one *marque* reigned supreme in the Grand Manner stakes—the Isotta-Fraschini, probably because of the tax structure under the Benito Mussolini regime. This was heavily loaded against cars of over 3 litres (the State-supported Alfa Romeo firm had a nice line in 2.9-litre cars) and helped to persuade Fiat to shelve a 6.6-litre straight-eight they were testing in 1931, with a view to production a year or so later.

Isotta-Fraschini was founded in 1900 by Cesare Isotta and Vincenzo Fraschini. They produced their first design in 1903. The designer of all their great cars was Giustino Cattaneo, who started with the company in 1905 and stayed until it ceased car production in 1935.

After the First World War he designed one model, the Tipo 8. This had a long-stroke eight-cylinder engine with pushrod-operated overhead valves and gave only 80bhp from nearly 6 litres. The company had patented four-wheel brakes in 1909 and this new car definitely needed this patent innovation. It had a wheelbase of some 12 feet and the weight of coach-work that this encouraged.

From the first, the Isotta-Fraschini was designed as a luxury machine for customers wealthy enough to employ a chauffeur. As a result the Isotta never gained the same sporting owner-driver reputation as the Hispano-Suiza. But this did nothing to harm its sales. About a third of the 1400 Tipo 8 cars produced were sold to America. They were bought by personalities such as Jack Dempsey, Clara Bow, Rudolph Valentino and Douglas Fairbanks senior, who all needed large, exotic 'foreign' cars—

Above: *An Isotta-Fraschini is 'Grand' by any standards; this limousine provided family motoring of a high order*

Right: *This open four-seater is a good example of the large tourers built by the Belgian Minerva company*

handsome machines that nevertheless cut a slightly sporting dash. In Europe, Isottas were bought by customers as different as Pope Pius XI, the Aga Khan and the King of Italy.

Cattaneo developed a new version of the Tipo 8, called the Tipo 8A. This had an increased engine size of 7332cc. Two specially-tuned versions, the Spinto and the Super Spinto, had as much as 155bhp available. The new models had deeper and stiffer chassis frames, bigger brakes and higher axle ratios, so that the Super Spinto could just top 100mph.

The Tipo 8A was sold between 1924 and 1931, when the 8B was introduced. Engine improvements increased the top speed yet again: the power output now climbed up to 160bhp at

Above: *The Rolls-Royce Silver Ghost was Britain's offering in the Grand Manner stakes before the start of the First World War*

Left: *The Rolls-Royce 'Ghost' spanned a number of years; its mechanical excellence was clothed in body styles as various as the two shown here*

3000rpm. An improved chassis with hydraulic shock absorbers should have made the 8B the most popular of all Isotta models, but by 1935 only 100 or so had been sold. The factory was taken over by the Caproni aircraft firm.

Like many of the large, long wheelbase leviathans, Isotta relied on the coach-builders for style and finished looks. However, times had changed and the number of people who could afford 'bespoke' bodies on such large cars was dwindling. Even Rolls-Royce had to accept that the days of cars designed specially for customers who had chauffeurs were passing. The owner-driver had to be catered for and motoring in the Grand Manner was on its way out.

Left: The famous Rolls-Royce radiator suggests only the best in motoring

Below: The French offered Grand Manner motoring with the Renault 'Forty-five' known as the 40CV in France. The Coupé de Ville (left) is a typical example. Smaller Renaults like the one on the right were excellent touring cars

Facing the Isottas in the museum and looking rather self-conscious, is a group of mundane Rolls-Royce saloons of the mid-1930s. They bear little or no comparison to the handsome Phantom Sedancas de Ville of the golden early 1930s, or to the Silver Ghosts from just before and after the First World War.

Perhaps the major reason behind the death of Grand Manner motoring was the financial burden of the Depression. Many of the smaller firms were killed off: larger ones were obliged to rationalise and mechanise production. As car ownership became more widespread, owners' requirements changed radically. Motoring was no longer sport for the aristocracy and upper classes. Public roads could no longer be their playground; indeed the roads had become truly public.

The car rapidly became simply a functional means of getting from place to place. The values by which cars were assessed were no longer those of the Grand Manner, where cost was of little importance and perfection was the sole criterion. Car owners wanted value for money—and the particular blend of comfort that depended on a flexible chassis, soft springing and low-geared steering.

The change in motoring may well be one reason why people began to collect cars instead of using them. While there are many reasons for collecting, prominent among them is the desire to re-live a lost age, perhaps recalling the delights of youth—or another aspect of the past which, in retrospect, seems particularly pleasant.

In their remarkable collection, the Schlumpf brothers present a picture of motoring from its inception to the point where it began to lose its individuality in favour of mass production. It is fitting that the latest cars in the collection are racing cars, the one area where generalisation has not yet taken a complete hold; where machines can be as idiosyncratic as the Schlumpfs.

Unlike many motor museums the cars in the Mulhouse collection appear much as they did when in daily use. They have been restored but have not been 'prettied up'.

The Schlumpf collection, like the story behind its acquisition, is firmly rooted in the reality of man's follies, triumphs, and improbable designs.

The Museum

The plan indicates where various motor cars are located

| | Lorraine | Delaunay-Belleville | Isotta-Fraschini | Farman | |

Austro Daimler

Early bicycles

Horch and Audi

Maybach

Daimler and Minerva

Lancia and Minerva

Rolls-Royce and Bentley
Silver Ghost, Phantom II and III

Panhard and Renault
from 1892 to 1930

de Dion Bouton and Delahaye

Early French cars
Zedel
Le Zebre
Rochet-Schneider
Pilain

Early French cars
Monet Goyen   Georges Richard   Esculape

Motorcycles and Tricycles   **Early French cars**   Fouillaron
Gladiator
Delage
Decauville

Lago-Talbot
Racing cars   **Ferrari**
Racing and sp

Bugatti
s 46 and 50
chassis
Hispano-Suiza

Bugatti
Type 43
chassis

Supercharger display

Bugattis
Type 46

Steam cars and Early cars

cedes-Benz
cars
3 SSK 300 SL
5 770 Grosser

Bugatti boat   **Bugatti engines**
Bugatti
Types 57S and 57SC
and Type 56

**Mercedes
cedes-Benz**

Veteran Benz cars

Bugatti
Type 57 and 57C
with Type 50, Type 64 and Type 101

Jacquot
Serpollet
racer

Peugeot
from 1912 to 1935

Bugatti
Royales
and
Type 46

Bugatti
Types 49, 44, 40 and 38

cellaneous French cars
Ballot racing car
Amilcar C6

Bugatti
Types 43 and 55
and Bugatti experimental cars
Types 68, 73, 252

Bugatti
Type 35T

Maserati
Porsche and Cisitalia

Factory Bugatti
Racing cars Types 45, 47, 51, 50B, 251

Dedication stand

**Alfa Romeo
and
Gordini**

Bugatti
Grand Prix
Types 32, 35, 37, 51

Ferrari 312B

Dufaux

Entrance

Lotus
Racing cars

Early Bugatti cars
'Garros'
BB   Type 28

We would like to thank the following individuals and organisations who supplied illustrations to the book:

Autocar: 138, 147, 151

Conway: 12, 16, 17, 20, 45, 48, 100, 108, 111, 114-115

Cramer: 61, 62, 65, 67, 72, 74, 77, 86, 104, 105, 117, 128, 140-141, 172, 176, 177, 178, 179, 182

David Hodges Collection: 38, 93, 94, 110

Gerrer: 12-13, 29, 31-32, 37, 53

Goddard: 99, 101, 102-103, 106, 110, 111, 114-115, 116, 146, 164, 165, 170-171, 173, 182

Hillmeyer: 34-35, 46, 47, 54-55, 57, 60, 63, 70-71, 75, 76, 77, 99, 102-103, 107, 110, 112, 116, 124-125, 126-127, 130-131, 132, 133, 134-135, 138, 139, 142, 148-149, 150-151, 154-155, 158, 159, 162, 163, 164, 174, 175

Lienhard: 12, 21, 24, 37, 40, 49, 51, 57, 58, 59, 62, 63, 64, 66, 69, 72, 74, 75, 76, 84, 88, 90-91, 98, 113, 114, 115, 118-119, 153, 162, 162-163, 171, 174, 179, 183, 184

Planet News: 140

Rowe: 58-59, 73, 82-83, 85, 86-87, 88, 90-91, 94, 94-95, 95, 96, 97, 122-123, 142-143, 147, 150, 154, 156, 163, 165

Schmitt: 31, 32, 33, 36, 42, 48, 49, 53

Schwobthaler: 21

Southern Railway System: 42, 44

Sunday Times: 46, 113, 171